ALLERGEN AWARENESS
A Chef's Prospective

by Myron "Keith" Norman
Executive Chef and Food Allergy Awareness Advocate

Cover and Interior Design: urickdesign.com

Photography:

ISBN: 978-0-9997232-0-3

COMMITMENT FROM INDUSTRY

The reality that lives are lost from eating certain food items should be motivation enough for training, advocacy and spreading awareness.

The number of food allergic guests rises each year. Considering the lives affected by life threatening food allergies, should bring front and center the need and importance for consistent and sustained measurable food allergy training. There is an urgent need for all food establishments to embrace awareness of food allergies, and the growing number of food allergic guests. The commitment for change must start with ownership and executive management. Training cannot be optional it must be mandatory, written and enforced throughout the food code.

Basic training and awareness must be a mandatory standard and starting point. It must be measurable, and it should lay the foundation for advanced awareness training and certification from a credentialed organization. Food Safety and Allergen training go hand in hand and must be mandatory for all levels of management and all service and culinary team classifications.

The lack of awareness and compliance throughout the hospitality industry has prompted many states to pass laws requiring food establishments to provide basic allergy training with emphasis on allergies, intolerances, celiac disease and sensitivities which have similar symptoms, similarities but are different. Many food establishments do not understand what a food allergy is. Mistaking life threatening food allergies with an intolerance or sensitivity is common, yet in my professional opinion it is best to treat life threatening food allergies, intolerances and sensitivities the same.

The laws also require food allergy awareness posters to be visible in food prep areas and language on menus to encourage the food allergic guest to make the server aware of the food allergy.

We all must work together to ensure that no life will be lost simply by eating a certain food item!!!

WHAT PEOPLE ARE SAYING...

Your stance on food allergic guests is wonderful! When you take time to help food allergic diners, you gain friends for life!

Kathy Lynn Maracle

Thank you so so much for being so accepting of food allergy customers! Eating out with my FA child really isn't an option because too many people see his needs as an inconvenience. We need more chefs with this perspective and they need to advertise it! The FA community is loyal to those willing to work with us and have so few reliably safe choices. Thank you so much for treating FA customers as normal customers!

Candace Morris Van Horn

I think most chefs would pay us to go away, due to the number of allergens in our profile! I'm sure plenty of others would enjoy the challenge though! And that's what makes Chef Norman awesome! Thank you for your advocacy and support!

Abigail Flavin

Every time I cook or make something that has to do with allergies I always remember how Chef Norman said "It's not what you do when everyone is looking, it's what you do when no one is around. Peoples lives are in your hands." You're an amazing instructor and role model for future and current chefs.

Tanesha Turner

You are amazing! Thank you for all you do for so many xoxo!

Rayna Jo Engle

I am proud to call you a friend. You have touched many hearts in your amazing presentation of food that is safe for our children. Thank you! You have touched my heart as well – you are a great man.

Linda Menighan

More and more of you is needed in this world. Your presence, your voice and your passion to bring awareness. You are saving lives, and effecting the world by being in it. So grateful for your concern to bring this very important issue to the forefront. You are effecting so many lives my dear friend, and wonderful man. A humanitarian with an enormous heart and so much wisdom. I thank you for making a difference! And for being the wonderful you that you are!

Lori Davis

I'm so excited! FAACT's Teen Retreat has always been my favorite allergy event. The fact that it's at South Point Hotel & Casino in Las Vegas is such an added bonus. That is the only place that my child can confidently order her food and rest assured it's safe. It's truly a vacation for me as a parent not to have to plan her meals and cook her food in our hotel room. Chef Keith Norman and his staff are truly amazing. If they can cook for my daughter, Kendall, they can cook for anyone! Spending time with families that are truly walking in your same footsteps is life changing. It's easy to feel alone or like "the helicopter parent" when raising a child with life threatening food allergies. Teen summit is a weekend that not only empowers your teens, but parents as well. I'm looking forward to spending time with my FAACT family and meeting new members.

Kim Bell Hollinger

ACKNOWLEDGMENTS

Father, I take this time to say thank you. Thank you for the opportunity to put words to paper in hopes that hearts and mind will open and allergy advocates will be born, Chefs will embrace allergens with an open mind and heart, and that those who live with food allergies on a daily basis will know that their lives matter. Amen.

To my mother, Gladys Mae Norman, who inspires me, who has sat on my shoulder and has been my angel for 52 years, I have missed you every year but I am thankful knowing that you have always been with me in spirit and song. RIP mom, I love you.

To my grandmother, Elizabeth Norman (Big Ma). Thank you for taking us in, in 1966. Your sacrifice, your commitment and your love will always be a burning light in our hearts, Officer Dibbles and Red Charlie would not be the men we are today without you. Rest In Peace.

To my grandfather Emory Lynch (Big Papa). There were many influences in my early life, but none that impacted who I have become more than you. I have fond memories of the times I would come to your garage and you would let me tinker with lawn mowers or other little things. I know now that the lawn mower would not start because you had the spark plug off. But after a few pulls and beads of sweat running down my face, I saw you put the spark plug wire on and when it started you said you did it. I will always remember your first words every time I would see you "how is your conduct." Those words have helped to shape the man that I have become.

To my brother Alonzo Norman (Lonnie), a true culinary genius. We grew up together in Big Ma's house, where we took cooking lessons from one of the absolute best Master Chefs ever. Learning how to make our first PB&J, our first fried bologna sandwich, and graduating to our first Thanksgiving dinner under Big Ma's watchful eye. Big Ma was the absolute best, thank you for sharing that experience and the love of cooking.

To my Meathead Skillet Biscuit (Matthew Patrick Norman), and my Pook Pook (Ashley Samantha Gayle Norman), my son and daughter. You inspire me with your smarts, your athletic ability and your big open and kind hearts. I love being your Pops, and especially love whooping you on the basketball court. I love everything there is to love about the two of you. The world is a better place because you both are in it. Love you bunches.

To Booh, one of my greatest lessons, one of my greatest joys. Truly "when the student is ready, the teacher will appear" thank you for you. Love you bunches. "When you change the way you look at things, the things you look at change." Dr. Wayne Dyer.

To Juliet, thank you for turning on the light my life-changing friend "HOLLLLA." "One of my greatest passions is striving to live my own absolute best life and express my greatest human potential." I'm in this journey with you! JS.

To Ms. Rayna, "I don't mind what happens, I embrace it!" Love you bunches!

PASSION, ATTITUDE, COMMITMENT AND KNOWLEDGE

A guest with food allergies is not an inconvenience or an interruption of service. For a Chef, patience, understanding and a willingness to go the extra mile to ensure that the life being entrusted to him or her, can dine in a safe environment and enjoy a wholesome meal that will not harm them.
Chef Keith Norman

CONTENTS

PART FIVE - ALLERGEN FRIENDLY RECIPES

PART SIX - ARTICLES AND APPEARANCES

FOREWORD

As parents of two food allergic children, we've seen our share of scary food experiences, to include physical, emotional, and psychological reactions. Fortunately, there are many champions willing to help with such challenges. One such champion is Chef Keith Norman.

We were blessed to cross paths with Chef Keith at the Food Allergy and Anaphylaxis Network (FAAN) conference in the Spring of 2010. Chef Keith made it clear on that day, and on every single day since, that Food Service professionals can absolutely make a positive impact on the lives of those dealing with food safety concerns. If you have food allergies, suffer from a food safety incident, are a food service professional, or a concerned parent like us, you will definitely benefit from Chef Keith's experiences.

Since our first chance encounter to this very day, Chef Keith demonstrates an unwavering commitment and relentless passion for making a difference in the community, and across the nation, to protect and serve others through his professionalism. He is a college food safety instructor, a regular speaker at food allergy and food safety events and a highly experienced chef who manages food safety for numerous restaurants. It is our hope that you embrace his passion for doing more for food safety and food allergies. Chef Keith can't do it alone, researchers estimate 15 million Americans have food allergies, therefore your help is needed too.

If you are ever fortunate enough to cross paths with Chef Keith, don't pass up the opportunity. He has a charming and engaging personality that will brighten your day.

While an imperfect substitute to meeting him, the next best thing is to benefit from his words in this book. Enjoy!

Chef Keith, it is our distinct honor to thank you for all you do for so many. Most of all we value your friendship. You are a blessing to all!

Sincerely,

Duane and Dana Gordin

Father and Mother of two children with potentially life-threatening food allergies to peanuts, various tree nuts, and shellfish. As well as FAAN, and later, Food Allergy Research & Education (FARE), volunteers and walk representatives.

I am particularly excited about the subject matter of Keith Norman's book. I've known Keith for twenty-eight years and his dedication and passion for the culinary arts has been noteworthy.

I share his unwavering commitment to Food Safety and Allergen Awareness. I encourage every Chef and restaurant owner to embrace this growing disability. *Allergen Awareness, a Chef's Perspective* is a "must read." It definitely provides the most necessary and mandatory tools for Chefs to properly serve food allergic guests.

Gustav Mauler
Certified Master Chef
Owner/Consultant
Spiedini Italian Ristorante

In Today's world, every major food operation, whether wholesale or retail, needs a Keith Norman. With all the known food allergies and health department regulations, it is imperative to have a knowledgeable person on staff. In my 50 years of operating restaurants and other food outlets, I have never found an individual more committed to protecting the customer and the establishment than Chef Norman. Every restaurateur should have a copy of this book.

Michael Gaughan
Owner
South Point Hotel, Casino, and Spa

ABOUT CHEF MYRON "KEITH" NORMAN

As a Veteran Marine, Chef Norman brings a sense of discipline and order to everything he does, both in business and in the culinary world, with over 20 years experience in the Hospitality and Service Industry.

Chef Norman has a passion for food safety and sanitation that is apparent in his role as Assistant Executive Chef and Food Safety Manager for the South Point Hotel & Casino and as a former culinary arts instructor at The International Culinary School at The Art Institute of Las Vegas. In both roles, Chef Norman is responsible for training and educating students and culinary professionals in one of the most important facets of the food service industry.

Chef Norman is the go-to chef with many food allergy resource organizations. He is highly trusted within the food allergy community.

He has worked his way up the culinary ladder at Las Vegas properties to include Bally's, the Mirage, Treasure Island, Paris, Suncoast and South Point hotels and casinos. He is a certified Master Allergen Awareness Trainer, certified professional food manager, certified HACCP (Hazard Analysis and Critical Control Points) manager, NEHA (National Environmental Health Association) certified food trainer, NRA (Nevada Restaurant Association) Servsafe Instructor/Proctor and subject matter expert, a certified registered OSHA (Occupational Safety and Health Administration) trainer and a master certified food and beverage executive.

Chef Norman sits on the Board of Directors for Stop Foodborne Illness, National Restaurant Association Education Foundation and Food Allergy & Anaphylaxis Connection

Team (FAACT). He is a member of the International Food Safety Council, Alliance of Black Culinarians, American Culinary Federation and the Nevada Food Safety Task Force – Nevada Environmental Health Association.

Awards and Recognition

2010 - Nominated for Culinarian of the year

2010 - Guest Speaker at the FAAN conference in Las Vegas

2010 - FAAN Walk for Food Allergy plaque in appreciation of volunteer activities

2011 - Emcee for Food Safety Day in Chicago

2011 - FAAN Walk for Food Allergy Las Vegas, NV Committee member

2012 - Guest Speaker for Nevada Food Safety Task Force Conference

2012 - FAAN Walk for Food Allergy Las Vegas, NV Honorary Chair

2012 - Nevada Humanitarian Award for Food Allergy's

2013 - Nominated for the National Restaurant Association Best Neighbor Award

2013 - Nevada Environmental Health Professional of the Year

2014 - FAACT National Conference and FAACT Teen Retreat Speaker

2014 - Food Allergen Blogger Conference Chef/Consultant

2015 - Food Allergen Bloggers Conference Chef/Consultant

2015 - FAACT Food Industry & Research Summit Speaker

2015 - FAACT Teen Retreat/Chef

2016 - Allergy & Asthma Network USAnaphylaxis Summit Speaker

2016 - FAACT Food Industry & Research Summit Speaker

2016 - FAACT Teen Retreat/Chef

2016 - FAACT Leadership Summit Speaker

2017 - AllerTrain Food Allergy Symposium for Industry Speaker

2017 - Nevada Food Safety Task Force/Nevada Environment Health Association Speaker

2017 - American Culinary Federation National Conference Speaker

A WORD FROM THE AUTHOR

With the encouragement from many of my family and dear friends, I share this book with you. Not only as a source of inspiration and encouragement, but I hope it will pull and tug at your heart strings. I hope at some point you will put yourselves in the shoes of those that I advocate for – not only in this book, but also through my attitude, my behavior, my knowledge and my unwavering commitment to ensuring that every guest with food allergies will be able to safely dine when eating out. And we as a band of culinarian brothers and sisters will continue to embrace the change, and become a bigger part of the conversation.

I am honored and humbled to look back on my Food Safety/Allergen Awareness journey over the last nine plus years, to know that I have made a difference, impacted lives and helped to begin the allergen conversation with this industry and its regulators. Yet this does not diminish the fact that there is so much more that needs to be done. To all of my adopted kids who are allergen warriors, I thank each of you for pushing me to learn more and to do more. To my allergen family moms and dads whom I have come to love over the years, thank you for allowing me to be a part of your stories, thank you for your trust, thank you for your love and friendship. Remember, we are in it to win it, and until we find a cure, or until science can answer the "why" question, we will just keep swimming.

As a proud father of two amazing young adults, an Executive Chef, Food Safety and Allergen Awareness Consultant, Mentor and Educator I am excited to share what I have learned over the years with every reader. I am honored to be recognized as a leader and trend setter in the allergy community, and humbled at the opportunities over the years to speak at local Nevada Schools, Nevada Environmental Health Association, Nevada Food Safety Task Force, Nevada ACF meetings, Southern Neveda Health District Industry Meeting, Allergen and Asthma Conferences, Food Allergen Bloggers Conference, FAACT's Food Industry & Research Summit, Leadership Summit, Teen Retreat and at the 2017 ACF National Convention.

Chef Keith Norman

Everyone has a story and at the end of the day it's just a story.
If you want different, change the story.
Emory Lynch Jr

PROFESSIONAL REFERENCES

Chef Keith, some 15 years after I met him, remains an inspiration to me and to so many others in the culinary community. Whether it is Chef's for Kids, homeless veterans, underprivileged kids that he can mentor, Keith never turns down an opportunity to help with ANY project that shares his wisdom, talent and love. Now Keith takes food safety and allergen awareness to a higher level with this wonderful book. These are not books that make it to the NY Times Best Seller List. They are written to push the envelope of awareness, to express a passion for a subject – and these subjects, food safety and allergen awareness, alter people's lives and not in a good way. Our industry DOES need to take heed. As a community, we are not doing a good enough job. It is my hope that Keith's book will alter the thinking of many food service personnel, because it is written by "one of us," not a food scientist, but by someone who lives this stuff every day on the job. Semper Fi my brother!

Ed Manley
President at Veteran's Suppport Network

Keith Norman is a very experienced food safety and quality assurance focused chef. This book, written in an easy to understand and implement manner, ensures that this important topic will be preserved and disseminated for years to come. Kudos to Keith for bringing joy to my heart over my life time work as well.

O. Peter Snyder, Jr., Ph.D.

Chef Norman has been a long-standing advocate for food safety education. He is an enthusiastic volunteer for high-school, post-secondary, and industry culinarians sharing his knowledge and expertise. Chef Norman is to be commended for his unending passion to create awareness and solutions to Allergen issues in our industry.

Katherine Jacobi, President & CEO
Nevada Restaurant Association/Educational Foundation

Chef Keith is my hero! He is so positive and so committed to food safety and issues related to food allergies. He is a great Chef, great man and I am happy to call him my friend. He has been a Board Member and Food Safety Advocate for Stop Foodborne Illness for over eight years. I am excited for his book as I know it will be an excellent read, reference and text book that addresses this growing disability. Well done Chef.

Deirdre Schlunegger
Chief Executive Officer
Stop Foodborne Illness

In my forty years in food service and culinary education, it is rare to have the opportunity to work with someone like Keith Norman. The passion he has for food safety and sanitation is contagious. He brings fun and excitement to a very serious topic. I am excited that Keith brings a fresh look at sanitation and emphasizes the growing need for allergen awareness. Keith was a joy to work with and I am thrilled to support and endorse Allergen Awareness, a Chefs Perspective.

David Hendricksen, CCE, CCC
National Culinary Director
The International Culinary Schools
At the Art Institute

I am excited for this much needed book, the impact that it will make cannot be measured. Knowing and having worked with Keith for over 17 years, his passion for changing lives through food safety and allergen advocacy is noteworthy. His dedication to the hospitality industry is only surpassed by his leadership & professionalism. Honored to call you my dear friend.

David Ross
CEO, Gaming Asset Management Advisers

Food safety was always something emphasized at my properties, but I did not give nearly enough thought to Food Allergies. That is until Chef Keith opened my eyes to so many individuals affected by them. Since then, our Allergen Program has become a great source of pride at the South Point. With 11 food outlets and 10,000 + meals a day, I sleep very well at night knowing our guests are safe thanks to Chef's diligence, knowledge, and training programs. It is not just a job for Chef Keith, it is a passion and thankfully, that passion seems to be contagious because it has spread across our entire property.

Ryan Growney
General Manager
South Point Hotel, Casino, and Spa

Food Safety is the foundation of any successful food and beverage operation. I have been a friend and colleague of Chef Keith Norman for almost thirty years and have been honored to have worked beside him building and managing food safety programs at the Suncoast and South Point that addressed training, food code compliance, a working relationship with the local health department and allergen awareness. I am excited for this much needed tool that shines a specific light on food allergies, thank you Keith for your friendship, dedication and commitment to raising the BAR.

Tom Jannarone
Corporate General Manager
Casa Blanca and Virgin River Hotel Casino and Spa

I have the honor and privilege of coming to work every day with Chef Keith. This Marine certainly knows how to improvise, overcome and adapt as it relates to the ever changing hospitality industry. His leadership, knowledge and dedication to life threatening food allergies is second to none. Keith is my partner here at the South Point as it relates to "Protecting the A" which refers to our grade cards from the health department. Keith understands that leadership is not about authority but influence. His constant training, evaluating and motivating of what our team does and how they do it is one of the main reasons why we continue to excel. To know Keith is to love Keith. He has never had a bad day. Just ask him. His smile is contagious and he is a friend to many and I am proud to say he is my friend. When I count the blessing in my life I count Keith twice.

Michael Kennedy
Director of Food Operations
South Point Hotel, Casino, and Spa

My daughter is an amazing athlete! When I played basketball in high school and the Marine Corp I wore #22. My daughter honored me with wearing #22 when she played ball in high school, at University of Texas and as a professional basketball player.

I am honored to dedicate this page to #22!!

When you open up the dictionary and look up "hard work" you'll see a picture of my "Pops". He relentlessly pursues his goals, many of which are centered around making other people's lives easier and safer. Words can't describe how happy I am for my Dad to be finishing his first book! He has a unique and special way of connecting with everyone that he meets, making each interaction memorable. He's always been an inspiration and a voice of reason in my life. I have lots of memories with my Dad, enough to fill a few books! One very special memory in particular sticks out. My brother and I went to a tiny private elementary school back in the day. The kitchen in the school cafeteria was tiny so whenever there were special events, my Dad would cater meals for the entire school! I remember being so proud when my Dad would walk into the cafeteria with his big white chef hat and his coat and all the other kids would run up and ask me if that was my Dad and I proudly say "Yes, that's my Dad! He's a chef!" I still run into people that I went to school with that ask about "Chef Keith." I'm just as proud of my Dad as I was that day.

I know that you and your family will enjoy this book for years to come!

Love you Pops!

Ashley Gayle

PART ONE

KIM HOLLINGER'S REAL LIFE STORY

Ordering from a server as a person with severe allergies, as well as being a parent of a daughter with severe allergies can be terrifying. My best analogy is that it's like handing an entire kitchen staff and wait staff loaded guns. Each and every person has a finger on the trigger, and they are all pointed at my child's head as well as my own. Through the years we have encountered some amazing people but that is usually not the case.

Every time we eat out, when I order our food I explain to the server that we have severe allergies. Once when eating out, I explained in detail that I have a severe pork allergy. This was the server's exact response: "Okay, so what part of the pig are you allergic to?" I answered with "the whole thing!". She replied "I know, but is it lactose intolerance or a milk allergy?" I said "No. I'm deathly allergic to pork, and my epinephrine auto-injector is right here! She acted like she understood and took my order."

Our food came and it was delicious until my tongue and lips started to swell, and then I began coughing and barking like a seal. I took my inhaler and injected myself with an Auto-Injector. My family went to go talk to the cook and learned he had never been told anything about my allergy. He cooked my eggs right along with the bacon using the same spatula. Obviously I survived, but it was a frightening ordeal that shouldn't have happened.

I share my story in hopes that you will commit to embracing the over 15 million Americans living with life threatening food allergies.

Another scary episode occurred when we were on vacation in San Diego, California. I called several days ahead, and spoke to the hotel food services manager regarding my daughter's unique situation. I was assured there weren't any peanuts in the facility. Our first night we were there swimming and dining poolside. My daughter's best friend & cousin were with us on the trip as well. After eating, the two other girls went to get in the pool, but I had Kendall sit back a few minutes to monitor a strange hive on her face. She was reluctant but agreed.

Within a few minutes my daughter went from a single hive to blue lips and losing consciousness. I injected her leg with an epinephrine auto-injector and yelled for 911 to be called. Hotel security brought oxygen. All the color had left her already pale face and she looked lifeless. This was the first time my husband (Kendall's father, Tim Hollinger) had witnessed her go into anaphylactic shock. He was frozen with fear, but I went into automatic pilot mode. I knew what needed to take place in order to save her life, and everyone had to be 100% on point so she was not exposed to another life threatening allergen in the mean time.

The paramedics and fire department arrived and started working on her. Her vitals let them know she was in dire need of more medication and a breathing treatment. Once she was stable enough for transport, the paramedics took her to the Children's Hospital Emergency Room. Her blood pressure was in the 20's and they were unable to get a vein for an IV because her veins had collapsed from her blood pressure being so low. It was a long night in the hospital watching and waiting, but Kendall was finally discharged the next morning.

The next day I was on a conference call with the food services manager, hotel general manager, and the entire wait staff who helped us that night. They had already been going over the events of the night prior, and none of them could figure out or trace back any food coming into contact with her long list of allergens. Her food was prepared in a separate area and precautions were taken. It wasn't until I was paying our tab while checking out of the hotel that I discovered the "smoking gun". I happened to look down into a trash can while signing my bill and noticed Chex mix. I asked the server where it came from, and she told me that during happy hour every table had a large margarita glass full of the mix. The mix contained peanuts, so the residue was everywhere. Believing there were no peanuts in the resort we let Kendall be a kid and freely touch the fish tanks, she had her face against the glass just before her dinner.

This is an example of why allergic parents ask these questions. It's not to be demanding or make any person's job harder. We are simply trying to keep our kids alive, included and safe. I can't begin to tell you the amount of times my server has rolled his or her eyes, or sighed under their breath.

After this occurrence we quit eating out with Kendall. If we went out we brought her food with us. It wasn't until Chef Keith gained Kendall's trust and began cooking for her at The South Point Hotel & Casino that she ate food from outside of our home. Going there is truly a vacation for us all. Watching her eat something she enjoys without anxiety or fear is such an amazing feeling.

I don't know why God spared Kendall's life that night, or after any of the other near death anaphylactic reactions she's had. So many families have buried their precious children and loved ones from the same situation. I believe God has a bigger purpose for Kendall's life. Maybe just by you reading her story it will save another life or lives. Please take food allergies seriously and put in the extra effort to ensure a safe and pleasant dining experience. I know it might not be easy but think of families like my own, and just know how grateful we are when it's done right. It means the world to us that for a couple of hours my family is just like every other family eating out and enjoying a meal. If you're reading this it shows you're interested in making a difference, and that alone makes this crazy world a better place. Thank you!

Kim Hollinger

EMBRACING A FOOD ALLERGIC GUEST

A food allergic guest may have one food allergy or multiple:

- Peanut
- Peanut, tree nut
- Peanut, tree nut, dairy
- Peanut, tree nut, dairy, egg
- Peanut, tree nut, dairy, egg, shellfish
- Peanut, tree nut, dairy, egg, shellfish, fish
- Peanut, tree nut, dairy, egg, shellfish, fish, soy
- Peanut, tree nut, dairy, egg, shellfish, fish, soy, wheat
- or Baby Aeverie who comes to dine for the first time. Peanut, tree nut, fish, shellfish, dairy, beans, celiac disease, banana's, kiwi, pineapple and latex

ALLERGEN ALERT		
Server		
Table # *27*		
Peanut ☒	Onion ☐	
Tree Nut ☐	Garlic ☐	
Fish ☐	Tomato ☐	
Shell Fish ☐	Peppers ☐	
Dairy ☐	Gluten ☒	
Eggs ☐	Corn ☐	
Soy ☐	Seasame ☒	
Wheat ☐		

Other Instructions: *Please separate food items*

"Allergen family interaction" and questions that test awareness.

Scenario One:

Customer: We have life threatening food allergies.
Food Server: We have allergens in our kitchen and can't guarantee anything.
Blank stare from Food Server.
Customer: Are you saying you can't serve us? Won't serve us? Won't try to make food safe? Or just trying to help us understand that you really have allergens present but will do your best to reduce risk? Maybe we should go somewhere else.

Allergen Aware Food Server Response:
Food Server: We have allergens in our kitchen and can't guarantee anything, but let me make my manager and chef aware, so we can look at safe options for you.

Scenario Two:

Customer: We've eaten here before, and enjoy the fish and chips. Can you ask the chef to confirm the recipe has not changed and does not contain *xyz*?
Food Server: Nothing has changed.

Customer: We need you to double check. Time to leave, this Food Server is not willing to ensure our safety.

Allergen Aware Food Server Response:

Food Server: We normally review any menu or recipe changes in our pre-shift meeting, but let me confirm with my chef!!

Scenario Three:

Customer: We are allergic to peanuts, tree nuts, sesame and poppy seeds.

Food Server: Nope, none of that in that dish.

Customer: Wrong answer, what we wanted to hear is let me confirm with the chef those items are not in the dish.

Allergen Aware Food Server Response:

Food Server: That menu item is free of peanuts and tree nuts, but give me a moment to confirm that there are no sesame or poppy seeds in the ingredients.

Scenario Four:

Customer: My son is allergic to peanuts and tree nuts.

Food Server: We don't use peanut oil.

Customer: Great, what about other nuts?

Food Server: We don't use peanut oil

Allergen Aware Food Server Response:

Food Server: We don't use peanuts or tree nuts in any of our dishes but let me confirm that with my chef. Was there a specific menu item that you were interested in trying?

Questions to ask:

- May I speak with the chef?
- What training have you had in regards to allergen awareness?
- Do you have an allergen program in place?
- May I see the ingredients label please?
- What other foods do you fry in the fryer?

- Do any of the ingredients have milk, egg or shellfish in them?
- Will you please use a clean pan to cook the meat and not the grill?
- Can you please cut fresh potatoes to make fries, and cook them in a frying pan instead of the fryer?
- Will you wash your hands before getting the drink for my son/daughter?

I've had the honor of knowing and working with Chef Keith for nine years. His dedication and commitment to food allergen safety, sanitation, and education is commendable. He has educated and trained his staff from the front of the house to the back of the house to where they have successfully managed and served hundreds of food allergy patrons at South Point Hotel & Casino's restaurants and during many conferences, and he has trained many of the Las Vegas hotel and casino food establishments throughout the years. Chef Keith goes above and beyond to ensure the safety of all patrons and the culinary students he educates. His passion for food safety and sanitation is apparent in all that he does. I've personally partnered with Chef Keith on numerous education initiatives, and he has served my son with multiple food allergies several times while in Las Vegas. I can't thank him enough for all he has done for my family and all of the families affected by food allergy and life-threatening anaphylaxis. He has truly left his handprint on many hearts! Every food establishment in the country should be educated by Chef Keith and FAACT!

- Eleanor Garrow-Holding, President & CEO
Food Allergy & Anaphylaxis Connection Team (FAACT)

Food Compliments!
Every year I come to the Southpoint Casino to attend & teach at the Glass Craft & Bead Expo. I want to compliment you on your effort & commitment to accommodating food allergies. When I travel food becomes a huge issue but when I come to the Southpoint I know I will eat well & not have to worry about reactions. Typically I will find a restaurant or particular dish that I don't react to and eat it for practically every

meal. That can get boring for me but very annoying for my friends. Now that you are so great at what you do I can eat everywhere and this year I practically did. We had Mexican, the cafe, sushi, burgers and fries, room service & even dairy free popcorn at the movies! Thank you! Thank you! Thank you!

Susan McGarry

KNOW THE FAACTS

Food Allergy Basics

- Food allergies affect approximately 15 million Americans, including 6 million children.

- A food allergy is an immune system response to a food the body mistakenly believes is harmful.

- When a person with food allergy eats the food, his or her immune system releases massive amounts of chemicals, including histamine, that trigger a cascade of symptoms that can affect the respiratory system, the gastrointestinal tract, the skin, and/or the cardiovascular system.

- There is no cure for food allergies.

- The prevalence of food allergies appears to be increasing among children under the age of 18, affecting approximately 2 students in every classroom.

- Although food allergy desensitizations are being studied, these are not yet proven treatments, so strict avoidance is the only way to prevent an allergic reaction.

- Managing a food allergy on a daily basis involves constant vigilance.

- Trace amounts of an allergen can trigger an allergic reaction in some individuals.

- Unfortunately, food allergy deaths do occur, even among persons with a history of mild reactions in the past.

- 9-1-1 must ALWAYS be called with every anaphylactic reaction.

Anaphylaxis

- Is a serious allergic reaction that comes on quickly and has the potential to become life-threatening.

- Symptoms can develop rapidly after exposure to an allergen, often within minutes and usually within 30 minutes. However, it can take up to 2 hours for symptoms to occur after exposure to a food allergen.

- Sometimes a second round (or "phase") of allergic reactions can occur after the initial anaphylactic reaction. This is called "biphasic anaphylaxis". A second reaction may happen as early as an hour after the first reaction or as long as 72 hours later (the average is 10 hours later) and can be less severe, as severe, or even more severe than the initial reaction.

- Must be treated immediately with epinephrine (adrenaline).

Prompt administration of epinephrine is crucial to surviving a potentially life-threatening reaction. Epinephrine has very few side effects. It is prescribed as an auto-injector device (Auvi-Q®, EpiPen®). For more information, and to download poster and plan go to:

http://www.foodallergyawareness.org/foodallergy/

Anaphylaxis: Signs and Symptoms Poster (page 34), and link below:

http://www.foodallergyawareness.org/media/educationresources/Anaphylaxis-Symptoms-Poster_FINAL%2009-2016_PDF.pdf

There are over one hundred known food allergies, but these eight account for 90 percent of all food allergy reactions:

- Peanuts
- Tree nuts (cashews, pecans, walnuts, etc.)
- Milk
- Egg
- Wheat

- Soy
- Fish (halibut, salmon, etc.)
- Shellfish (crab, lobster, shrimp, etc.)

However, almost any food can cause a reaction.

- Must be treated immediately with epinephrine (adrenaline).
- To learn more about food allergy, we recommend the video "Understanding Food Allergy" by the National Institute of Allergy and Infectious Diseases.

A food allergy is NOT:

- A food intolerance (lactose intolerance, etc.).

    - An intolerance does not involve the immune system – it involves the digestive system because the body lacks an enzyme needed to digest and process a particular food.

    - Symptoms of an intolerance include gas, bloating, and abdominal pain.
- A food preference (vegetarian, kosher, etc.).
- Celiac Disease (autoimmune disease).

Avoid high-risk types of restaurants

Persons with food allergies should generally avoid high-risk types of restaurants, including:

- Buffets and deli stations (risk of cross-contact).
- Asian cuisine (peanuts, tree nuts used in many dishes).
- Bakeries (risk of cross-contact).
- Ethnic (language barrier).
- Delis
- Concession stands/hot dog carts
- Banquet/catering style events

Minimize risk

There are ways to minimize risk of accidental exposures and feel more secure about eating out.

- Look for allergy information from the restaurant. Some chains are food-allergy aware and may post allergen information on their website.

- Call and speak with the Manager or Chef prior to your visit.

- Ask if there is an allergen specific menu available.

- Ask to speak with the Chef to talk through the preparation of the meal.

- Consider using a "chef card" to alert the staff about your food allergy.

- Make the host/hostess and server aware of all known allergies upon arrival and before the order is taken.

- Leave the restaurant or bring your own food if you feel uncomfortable about the restaurant's food preparation.

- For more information about food allergies, contact FAACT, and visit FAACT's Education Resource Centerfor FREE and downloadable resources.

A parents greatest joy is their children; I am humbled and honored to share my son with all of the readers of this book. A wonderful son and athlete, and I have had the pleasure of watching him grow into an amazing young man. Keep living the dream and changing lives my son (AKA) Meathead Skillet Biscuit.

I am very happy for my pops and his new book because he is somebody who is pursuing his dreams every single day of the week. He is one of the hardest working individuals that I know, and I cannot wait to witness the success he creates for himself. A humble, generous man whose mission has always been to put others before himself. My pops is an inspiration to me, and the wonderful people he meets every single day. This book is a symbol of my pops' passion as he has poured all of his love and energy into educating individuals about the seriousness of food allergies. I am very proud of my pops, as I always hear wonderful stories from friends and family about how he has inspired them or motivated them to continue living life. The best part of all, is that I get to experience my pops every single day of the week, which is one of the best gifts anybody could ever ask for.

Matt Norman

SIGNS AND SYMPTOMS OF ANAPHYLAXIS

Anaphylaxis (an–a–fi–LAK–sis) is a serious allergic reaction that comes on quickly and has the potential to become life-threatening. The most common anaphylactic reactions are to foods, venom, medications, and latex.

Anaphylaxis signs and symptoms that may occur alone (*) or in any combination after exposure to an allergen include:

MOUTH:
itching, tingling, swelling of the lips/tongue/palate (roof of the mouth)

*THROAT:
hoarseness, tightening of throat, difficulty swallowing, hacking cough, stridor (a loud, high-pitched sound when breathing in)

*LUNGS:
shortness of breath, wheezing, coughing, chest pain, tightness

GUT:
abdominal pain, nausea, vomiting, diarrhea

CNS/BRAIN:
anxiety, panic, sense of doom

EYES/NOSE:
runny nose, stuffy nose, sneezing, watery red eyes, itchy eyes, swollen eyes

SKIN:
hives or other rash, redness/flushing, itching, swelling

*CIRCULATION/HEART:
chest pain, low blood pressure, weak pulse, shock, pale blue color, dizziness or fainting, lethargy (lack of energy)

* IMMEDIATE & POTENTIAL LIFE-THREATENING SYMPTOMS

Consult with a board-certified allergist for an accurate diagnosis and management plan.

- Although the majority of individuals experiencing anaphylaxis have skin symptoms, some of the most severe cases have no rash, hives, swelling

- **EPINEPHRINE is the first-line of treatment for anaphylaxis**

- Antihistamines, inhalers, & other treatments should only be used as <u>secondary</u> treatment

- ALWAYS CARRY TWO (2) epinephrine auto-injectors at all times

- When you, or someone you know, begin to experience symptoms, CALL 9-1-1 IMMEDIATELY!

FAACT
Food Allergy & Anaphylaxis
Connection Team
AWARENESS • ADVOCACY • EDUCATION
www.FoodAllergyAwareness.org

(513) 342-1293
Fax (513) 342-1239
P.O. Box 511
West Chester, OH 45071
info@FoodAllergyAwareness.org

The Voice of Food Allergy Awareness

10 FAACTS *about* Food Allergies

1. Food allergies affect approximately **15 million** Americans. Studies report that **1 in 13** children in the United States have a food allergy. This averages to **two** children per classroom.

2. A food allergy is an **immune system response** to a food that the body mistakenly believes is harmful.

3. Eight foods account for 90% of all food allergy reactions: **Peanuts, Tree nuts, Milk, Egg, Wheat, Soy, Fish, & Shellfish**. However, almost any food can cause a reaction.

4. There is **no cure** for food allergies and **strict avoidance** is the only way to prevent an allergic reaction.

5. **Trace amounts** of an allergen can trigger an allergic reaction in some individuals. Past reactions to a food allergy **do not predict future reactions!** Someone can still have a life-threatening reaction to a food they are allergic to, even if they have never had a serious reaction before.

6. Symptoms can **develop rapidly** after exposure to an allergen, often within minutes and usually within 30 minutes. However, it can take up to 2 hours for symptoms to occur after exposure to a food allergen.

7. Anaphylaxis is a **serious allergic reaction** that comes on quickly and has the potential to become life-threatening. Anaphylaxis requires immediate medical treatment, including an injection of epinephrine and a visit to the emergency room.

8. It is important to be deliberate and not hesitate when you have to use epinephrine. The device is **potentially life-saving**. A call to 9-1-1 and a trip to the emergency room should always follow epinephrine administration.

9. Individuals at risk should carry **two epinephrine auto-injectable devices** with them at all times AND an **Allergy and Anaphylaxis Emergency Care Action Plan** signed by a board-certified allergist.

10. **Food allergies continue to rise** – especially among children – and are a safety and public health concern across the United States. You can get free resources and find out how to help keep those with food allergies safe at:

www.FoodAllergyAwareness.org

FAACT
Food Allergy & Anaphylaxis
Connection Team
AWARENESS • ADVOCACY • EDUCATION
www.FoodAllergyAwareness.org

Food Allergies?

Preventing Cross-Contact and Accidental Environmental Exposure

Cross-contact and environmental exposure are often cited as top concerns for families managing food allergies. Cross-contact can occur through incidental contact with utensils, pots and pans, and preparation surfaces.

Environmental exposure can occur through contamination of surfaces and are widely thought to occur through inhalation of allergen. This is a particular concern at school and on airplanes. The good news is that allergens can be readily cleaned from hands and body parts, cookware and utensils, and environmental surfaces.

Tips to prevent environmental contamination:

When cleaning surfaces (such as desks, counters, tables, airline seats or tray tables, etc.), use a wipe that contains a commercial detergent (e.g., Clorox®, Lysol®, etc), or apply a spray-on detergent (e.g. Formula 409®, Fantastic®, Windex® Multi-Surface, etc.) and vigorously wipe the area that has come into contact with the allergen. **In a 2004 study, dish soap did not remove peanut allergen.**

Run contaminated pots, pans, and utensils through a normal dishwasher cycle or wash them by hand with hot, soapy water and scrub the surfaces thoroughly. Use a sponge, scouring pad, or dish rag that has not come into contact with the allergen. Rinse and dry thoroughly with a clean towel. Avoid just wiping down a knife or common utensil with a rag after touching an allergen (a common practice at sandwich shops).

For washing hands or face, use warm/hot, soapy water or a commercial "tidy" wipe. **Hand sanitizing gel is not sufficient to remove allergens.** This is important in the healthcare setting, as most healthcare facilities have moved to near-exclusive use of hand sanitizing gels for infectious purposes.

#KnowTheFAACTs
www.foodallergyawareness.org

Anaphylaxis FAACTs

1 Is a **serious allergic reaction** that comes on quickly and has the potential to become life-threatening.

2 **Symptoms** can develop rapidly after exposure to an allergen, often within minutes and usually within 30 minutes. However, it can take up to 2 hours for symptoms to occur after exposure to a food allergen.

3 Sometimes a second round (or "phase") of allergic reactions can occur after the initial anaphylactic reaction. This is called **"biphasic anaphylaxis"**. A second reaction may happen as early as an hour after the first reaction or as long as 72 hours later (the average is 10 hours later) and can be less severe, as severe, or even more severe than the initial reaction.

4 Must be treated immediately with **epinephrine** (adrenaline). Prompt administration of epinephrine is crucial to surviving a potentially life-threatening reaction.

#KnowTheFAACTs
www.foodallergyawareness.org

FAACT
Food Allergy & Anaphylaxis
Connection Team
AWARENESS • ADVOCACY • EDUCATION

NEWLY DIAGNOSED WITH
FOOD ALLERGIES?

The team at **FAACT** is here to support you as you learn to live a food-allergic lifestyle and manage your food allergy. Visit us at:
www.FoodAllergyAwareness.org

Avoid the Allergen

Assume nothing! Verify all ingredients before declaring a food item safe to eat. Read labels on packaged goods and if you have a question on the safety of a product, call the company directly. Learn how to clean potentially cross-contaminated surfaces...including your hands.

Be Prepared

Always have emergency medication (e.g., auto-injectable epinephrine and antihistamines) with you. Become familiar with how to use your epinephrine device and the steps in your emergency care action plan.

Consult a board-certified allergist

Allergists have specific training and expertise in food allergy and anaphylaxis diagnosis and management. Work closely with your board-certified allergist to better understand food allergy, the testing process and diagnosis, and to develop a management care plan.

#KnowTheFAACTs

PART TWO

BECOMING A CHEF

Big Ma's Kitchen

It was always a treat looking forward to the holidays each year, and the good home cooking that always brought family and friends to Big Ma's house. Everything was made from scratch, and you could see the love that went into each dish. It was always a special treat during canning season. My brother and I would take turns turning the handle of the manual grinder that attached to the kitchen table. We would have already prepped the fresh onions and peppers that would go into what my grandmother called "Cha

Cha". We would spend hours helping my grandmother with the canning duties right before winter. First filling the mason jars, and then on the stove for a water bath – what a beautiful time.

The patience and love that went into every pinch and every dash, Big Ma would joke when I would ask what was the secret, what made her food taste so good, she would occasionally reply, "It's the big toe" or "the dirty sock" that was added for flavor. The meals were simple – no fancy herbs, spices or oils, just a whole lot of love, patience and the perfect mix of garden fresh vegetables that made her food delicious.

Life as a Marine

One Saturday in June 1980, my friends Stan and Terry decided to join the Marine Corp. After learning that we could go in under the buddy system where we would all be in the same platoon, it seemed like a great idea. I believe my grandmother knew all along that

I was up to something. We were gone most of the day getting physicals, taking tests and then swearing in. After returning home my grandmother greeted me at the door with "You signed up for the service." I said yes. I'm not sure if that disappointed her, but I guess after raising me from age four, and now having kids myself I understand that look. High school graduation came and the next day I was off to Beaufort, South Carolina to the MCRD Parris Island (Marine Corp Recruit Depot) Platoon 2040. What a shocker! Yet as time went on I settled, and thirteen weeks later I graduated as a United States Marine.

Coming home after Boot Camp is hard to describe – everyone looked at me much differently. I had seen that look before, having three brothers who had joined the Marine Corp. That look of "Wow, we are proud of you". I will never forget that thirteen week transformation from "Oh shit, what did I get myself into?" to "Wow!"

I had many great moments as a marine – amazing military dashes, wonderful people and living in beautiful places. It was a humbling experience being a member of one of the United States' incredible fighting forces. The brother- and sisterhood cannot be explained with words – it is an overwhelming life long feeling.

My first duty station, where my professional culinary career began, was Marine Corp Air Station Cherry Point, North Carolina. I had never been on my own before, and it was nice looking at life through a different lens. After settling in, I met my Chief Cook GySgt Lasodi. He was firm but I came to learn that he was also fair, **that** was a huge lesson for me.

After a year at Cherry Point I was fortunate enough to be transferred to Kaneohe Bay, Hawaii – a beautiful place, but very hot and humid. After I settled in, I reported to the Main Dining Facility where I would meet my Dining Facility Manager, Gunnery Sergeant Roy Mullins. Gunny Mullins was dressed in a Hawaiian Chefs Jacket, white pants and black shiny boots. I visited with Gunny Mullins, took a tour of the dining facility and met my Chief Cook and new team.

After three Westpac Deployments and three amazing years in Hawaii, I received orders to Okinawa, Japan for one year. After which I was honored to attend Marine Security Guard School in Quantico, Virginia. During the next three years of my career I was fortunate to meet some amazing Marines and fellow service men and women, attend and participate in some amazing career building exercises along with life changing educational opportunities. After my tour in Virginia, I was pleased to hear that I would be reunited with my dear friend Master Sergeant Mullins. I received orders to Marine Corp Air Station El Toro, California. It was good seeing my friend and having another opportunity to make a difference. After two great years of working with Master Sergeant Mullins at both Dining facilities 364 and 322 at El Toro, I ended my eight year active duty and two year reserve Marine Corp career, and decided to relocate to Las Vegas. I lost my dear friend and Marine Corp Brother in 2017, RIP Master Sergeant Mullins.

Las Vegas Experience

First stop was the Union House to get referrals for open jobs. In three weeks I must have put applications at over thirty places, 7-11, grocery stores and hotels, yet no one called. I was frustrated, but determined, so I didn't give up. I remember going out on the last referral from the Union — it had been over a week, so I decided to call. Ms. Diane answered the phone and I said I was just following up. A week later I received a call from Bally's asking me to come in for an interview. I met with Chef Warner who while reading my application, gave me that look — the same look that I had gotten when I returned from boot camp. I was a Marine and carried myself as such. He hired me on the spot, and I started that night on the graveyard shift in the Coffee Shop with Chef Ernie. My Las Vegas culinary career was on its way.

A year later, I had worked my way to day shift. Around this time news of a new hotel and casino was being built, and was scheduled to open in 1989. I applied and was offered a position as a Master Cook at the Café by Executive Chef Ken Weicker. Though it was a fast paced environment, we did everything with style and grace. It was a joy experiencing my very first grand opening of a major casino, I felt blessed to have the opportunity to work with a Certified Master Chef (Gustav Mauler) and an amazing owner like Mr. Steve Wynn.

Challenges and Life Lessons

1992 and 1993 were difficult and challenging years for me. In 1992 I lost my sister and dad within a few weeks of each other, and in 1993 I lost Big Ma. Though I am thankful for great friends and family, and many amazing words of encouragement, my job performance, unfortunately, began to suffer. I was missing work and not supporting the team. Chef Ken called me to his office. I wasn't sure what he would say, as he was a straight faced, quiet kind of person. I sat down and he gave me the talk, "Bad things happen to good people, but you've gotta get back on the horse." – which is exactly what I needed at that time and I am still riding.

After four wonderful years and a promotion to the Buffet Chef, Mr. Wynn opened his next casino – Treasure Island. I was called in to Chef Ken's office and offered the position as Buffet Chef at the new property, so I embarked on my second major casino opening in 1993. What a special time, beautiful hotel, and an amazing opening team.

Moving through the ranks, I have always excelled and strived to be a better me in all areas of my life. Working for Mr. Wynn was amazing but working with Chef Ken who is certainly a dear friend was a plus for my career. After being successful in the Coffee Shop and Buffet environments, I wanted more so I asked Chef Ken what I needed to become his assistant. That is a question anyone seeking a promotion should ask their boss. He encouraged me to get Banquet experience. After 11 years with Treasure Island and the Mirage Resorts, I took an Assistant Banquet Chef position at Paris Hotel and Casino, which would be my third major resort opening. After obtaining banquet experience, I moved to the night Chef position, overseeing production and the Cook and Chill Program, which added valuable tools to my toolbox.

In early 2000, I received a call from my friend Chef Ken Weicker. We met for breakfast and he mentioned a new project, a new Casino, a new opening, a new opportunity. He offered me a position as his Assistant Executive Chef – so on to the Coast family I went. Along with an amazing team we would open the Suncoast Hotel Casino and Spa.

If you conduct a search for Food Safety professionals, one of the first names that will appear is Keith Norman. Keith has become a trusted leader and trend setter in the areas of food safety and allergen awareness.

Keith is a dear friend and worked for me for nearly two decades at the Mirage, Treasure Island and Suncoast Hotel Casino and Spa. In the early 2000s, I tasked Keith to teach our 400+ Food and Beverage staff how to wash their hands and to bring the food and beverage department into food code compliance. This was not a easy task, but the dedication, commitment and effort that Keith put into transforming and creating a food safety culture was noteworthy. Over the years, Keith continually raised the bar and expanded the training to cover all areas of Food Safety, HAACP, and Allergen awareness.

When you put on the Chef coat, guests expect to receive food that is safe. I am excited for Keith and I know that years of experience has gone into making the information in his book relevant. I am confident that Allergen Awareness, A Chef Perspective, will provide necessary tools for all Chefs where food allergic guests can enjoy meals without hesitation.

Chef Keith took a small and simple task and grew it into a very important aspect that will impact our profession for years to come.

Kenneth J Weicker CEC

Time for a Change

As my time at the Suncoast ended, I embraced my next experience at the South Point Casino and Resort, which is located on the south end of the Strip, where I am currently working. Fast forward to present, and the main inspiration for writing this book – it is my hope that reading this book will not only inspire every Chef, but to also tug at the heart strings of every culinarian, non food allergic family, every educator, every policy maker at every level of government, every restaurant and eatery worldwide that serves a food allergic guest.

ONE IMPORTANT PART OF BEING A CHEF

Being in the Service of Others

While still in high school, as a way to get the last three credits my brother and I needed to graduate, we took a Culinary Course. Being more focused on the three credits than the class, we were pleasantly surprised by this enjoyable experience. In our school kitchen, Ms. Lockert and Mr. Perchell ran the program. Ms. Lockert instilled in us the passion for cooking, creating new dishes and relying on team work. She was demanding in the kitchen, and made every guest feel special – giving new meaning to the phase "Hospitality". We lost Mrs. Lockert in 2017, but the lessons live on.

Now special dietary needs have become a huge part of Hospitality. Hospitality is the quality or disposition of receiving and treating guests or strangers in a warm, friendly and generous way. Regardless of what we call it – hospitality, guest service, customer service or patron service, at the end of the day every special needs guests have the right to dine safely. To achieve this, we must change the culinary and hospitality conversation by changing:

- Our attitudes towards guests with special needs
- Our commitment towards guests with special needs

- Our knowledge and awareness towards guests with special needs

- Our willingness to embrace and change our work environment

Imagine putting the life of your child or someone you love in the hands of another.
TW

We must strive to create an allergen aware culture that embraces these growing disabilities. To add to the definition of HOSPITALITY, with my commitment and knowledge, I create an experience for my food allergic guests through a genuine attitude that demonstrates my desire to give excellent quality, efficient service and a safe meal.

Chef Keith

Persevere

I have been honored over my career to do many things. One was teaching at one of the best culinary schools, The Art Institute. I enjoy seeing the awesome impact of adding heart and commitment to the curriculum. I enjoyed teaching, mentoring and had the honor of adding valuable resources to my students' tool boxes. As a Chef and educator, it is humbling to see your students graduate and become hospitality professionals. I always want to make sure everybody feels like they are somebody.

Over my nine of years of teaching, I can share many student success stories, but I must share one amazing never-give-up, you-can-do-it story. One semester, on the first day of class, I reviewed my roster and as the students entered class I greeted them, took roll call, and then went over the expectations for the next 11 weeks. Ms. Gladys, who clearly was an older more seasoned student, mentioned that she had not been in school for some time, and was unfamiliar with the computer which most of the students used. She said she didn't even know how to turn one on. I told her that I didn't either, and we chuckled. I told Ms. Gladys that I would work with her an hour before and after class. I did this for the first five weeks and then I paired her with a student much better then I with computers. My point is never giving up, and you are never too seasoned. Unfortunately, Ms. Gladys had two strokes during the school year, but she persevered and returned to school and graduated with her Bachelors Degree.

Failure

Failure is a necessary part of all growing experiences, and one that motivated me to be more pro-active in my early career. While stationed in Hawaii, I was getting ready for promotion to the rank of Sergeant. I was a good leader, and had obtained the rank as a Corporal fairly quickly. I studied hard, my physical fitness scores were in the high 290s, and I was an expert marksman. I knew everyone seeking promotion, and felt I was equally qualified. Yet I underestimated, and took for granted, the amount of time it would take to break down a fifty caliber machine gun, and then put it back together again. It was not a weapon I regularly used, but I had ample time to practice. I broke it down maybe a dozen times. In hind sight I should have broken it down *and* put it back together two hundred times! Needless to say, I was not promoted. It's ok to fail, but get back up, dust yourself off and move on.

The only stumbling block is the fear of failure. In cooking, you have to have a "what the hell" attitude.
Julia Childs

Leadership

There are many good chefs out there – chefs that can go into a kitchen and create master pieces. But being a great chef requires more than just technical proficiency – it requires leadership skills well above the norm, it requires a social skill set where your presence inspires others to be their best. It means managing long hours and multiple personalities while maintaining the appropriate attitude. We lead, we staff, we motivate to a common goal of excellence – in skill, in teamwork, in attitude all the while ensuring that at the end of everyday regardless of the days snapshot, your team knows that you appreciate, you value, and no matter what, you have their backs.

You must be open to making mistakes yourself, as well as your staff making mistakes. Listen, listen and listen because your staff speaks. Don't be afraid to make mistakes, that's how we learn, remember what our parents told us, that bit of advice has been handed down from generation to generation and how amazed we are when what our parents told us actually works. One of our greatest Chef Educators once said "The duty of a good Cuisinier is to transmit to the next generation everything he has learned and experienced." Ferdinand Point

Allergen Challenge – Daunting but Doable

I have been trained over the years by the very experts that live allergens on a daily basis, I have looked in the eyes of parents who have lost loved ones. I have seen the fear in a baby's eyes when I extend my hand to say hello, and she quickly pulls her hand away, because she is not sure what I may have touched. I have seen the same fear in a baby's eyes when I put a meal in front of her, and for a split second she defaults to the multiple times she has been resuscitated after eating something she's allergic to. These babies have become not only my teachers, but they have become my family. Qualifications go far beyond the amount of times you have served a food allergic guest, far beyond training and certification, far beyond

policy, procedures or allergen standard operation procedures. The most important qualification is managing food allergies and embracing the fear. When you do that, your food allergic guest, who is now placing their life in your hands, is no longer just a guest with food allergies. Preparing their meal becomes more than just preparing their meal, you talk different, you walk different, you think different and the heart beats with an unexplainable rhythm and you realize, that you are different.

My responsibility as a Chef, Food Safety Expert and Allergen Advocate is multi-leveled. In 2008 I would meet a young lady who was a 2006 victim of E.coli foodborne illness. My friend Rylee had eaten contaminated spinach and would endure what no nine year old should ever have to experience from eating food. When I met Rylee along with her parents, and heard her story, the life changing experience accelerated my commitment to food safety and advocacy. As a Chef I must continue to educate myself to ensure that I remain on the cutting edge. It is my responsibility to educate others tirelessly until every culinarian makes the shift, until every restaurant and food service institution speaks with one understanding – that food allergic guests lives matter. I advocate to create an allergen culture, bringing real life experience to the table, creating a movement of heart centered passion, attitude and commitment which gives every Chef and Culinarian the opportunity to pause and step into the shoes of that guest, whom with fear in their heart, has just entrusted their life to you.

When you love many with life threatening food allergies, it becomes personal, and no longer seen as a challenge. For me it is a way of life as a Chef, a family member, a friend and an allergen advocate.

Chef Keith Norman
FAACT Board of Directors

Allergens are not new. Allergens have been documented since 375 BC when Hippocrates, the father of medicine, gave the first description of an allergy to cheese. King Richard (1452-1485) among one of the first diagnosed with a strawberry allergy, and one of the first allergen fatalities documented in the early 1900.

FAAN

Times have changed since 2009 when I began my journey of changing the culture at the South Point. Back then there was quite a bit of push back, which I attributed to lack of awareness. I had attended multiple allergen conferences and reached out to FAAN (Food Allergy & Anaphylaxis Network), which is an organization that prides itself on allergen awareness, advocacy and raising the bar for restaurants and the public. They were very helpful in providing the tools needed to take my team to new levels of awareness.

My first experience with FAAN was attending and participating as a guest speaker at my first conference. I was overwhelmed to be a part of this experience, and to hear the stories from families, witnessing the fear, seeing the faces and challenges first hand. This was a defining moment for me and I knew then that I would do everything in my power to change the conversation and raise the bar on awareness in the culinary environment. After the morning sessions, I was placed on the panel listening to small children talk about their allergies and their fears of dying. Zac Chelini whom was also on the panel, spoke of a childhood memory where his friends smeared peanut butter on his face because they wanted to see what would happen. This heart wrenching story has stuck with me all of these years. It has been an honor and a privilege to watch Zac aadvocate for change. I am humbled to call him my friend and mentor.

Kendall

When I met Kendall in 2012, I only knew that I had just met an amazing young lady with multiple allergies. I did not realize that this young lady would change my life forever. When we met I knew we had an instant bond. I believe in my heart that Kendall knew that I would keep her safe. The first time I met her, she and her family were dining at one of the South Point restaurants. I asked her to walk with me, and I took her into the kitchens and introduced her to the team. I then gave her a rundown of what we had done in regards to the training and preparation for her visit. When we returned to the table where mom and dad were sitting, mom had a peculiar look on her face – I thought I had done something wrong. Mom said it was the first time Kendall had trusted any one enough to go off without her.

The always amazing
Chef Keith Norman!
This guy is a rock star!
Kendall Hollinger

Five years ago I walked into a restaurant, and as usual, refusing to eat, due to millions of close calls with my food allergies. Everyone had told me through my advocacy work for about a year of "The Amazing Chef Keith" and how I could safely eat at his restaurant. If I am being honest I walked into that restaurant with NO intention of eating that night. I was there at The South Point Hotel traveling for an advocacy engagement and I did not feel like taking any trips to the emergency room. Usually, my family members are the first ones to say "Hey let's not risk it". But this time they were trying to convince me. I found it so incredibly annoying when they threw me under the bus. The Chef came to our table and I was scared out of my mind. The difference between most restaurant staff and this one, was that this man CARED so much when he didn't have to. He saw my fear from food almost being deadly to me so many times, and he thought of me as being one of his own kids with this condition, so he found empathy. He offered to take me on a tour of the kitchen, which is like my worst nightmare! Inside my head I was thinking yeah that's great since that's where the food is! However, I had no idea what I would experience. All over the walls in this kitchen were signs with warnings and protocols for how to handle dietary restrictions. The kitchen was SO clean and everything that could harm me was SO separate from the area my food would even touch. I was in shock, I had never ever seen anything like this. I took a chance that day, praying before the food came as usual, and I am SO glad that I did. It may seem silly to most, but having my own hot plate of food at a restaurant was the best thing ever. Throughout the years Keith has become a friend and mentor in my life. I am SO grateful for humans like him who care so much about things that don't even effect them. Not only is his food SERIOUSLY YUMMY, but it's safe for people who don't have a choice but to be scared of one bite taking their life. I love you so much Keith! So glad God placed you in mine and my family's path! It's been such a joy to not only experience your kindness but get to see other kids I mentor and friends of mine get to eat safely at your restaurant!!! I am forever grateful for the heart you possess and the change you're making in so many lives. Because of you I now feel confident when walking into a restaurant, and deciding whether or not I should eat there, and I know there's always a safe place to go, even if it's in Vegas!!!

Kendall Hollinger

UNDERSTANDING THE FEARS OF GUESTS WITH FOOD ALLERGIES

With knowledge comes foundation, this must include stepping into a food allergic guests' shoes – seeing the situation through their eyes. Understanding the total life style change that the food allergy has caused. Often the team has not experienced food allergies so it may be necessary to approach it like any other life threatening disease, like cancer or heart disease, making the experience a bit more real. It's important to change the way the team looks at the food allergic guest. They must embrace the fact that this guest is afraid; this guest does not trust them, and is placing their life or the life of a loved one in their hands. At first this may be overwhelming, but once the team views the guest as a life that matters, and not just another customer, they will embrace going the extra mile to keep them safe, therefore the extra work will not be an inconvenience, but a way of life.

CHALLENGES AND RISK TAKERS

Challenges When Embracing A Food Allergic Guest

Often they are embarrassed or even intimidated by their allergen. They may feel that they have no reason to share their allergen, so how dare the server ask "are there any allergens or dietary concerns that I need to be aware of?" They may hear "Are you calling me fat? It's none of your business!", or "Why are you asking me?" In their minds ordering around the allergen has always worked, so they look for the simple menu items, not realizing that there are many steps to keeping them safe. The staff must take notice of the guests' order, and the 'buzz words' that should automatically prompt them to ask if there is an allergy or dietary concern that they should be aware of. We may need to be firm with this guest. This guest may feel embarrassed or uncomfortable because the server asked this question in front of their friends, or their date, therefore may become angry or agitated. The staff must embrace this guest in a positive way, because as this guest and his or her friends become aware that we are trying to keep them safe everything will make sense, and they will become more receptive to the question – not viewing it as an attack.

New Allergies

The newly diagnosed guest is still in shock so the server must be empathetic. They are learning, overwhelmed at the drastic life change, and they may not be fully aware of the consequences so often they trust too soon. Servers must be empathetic, patient and understanding. One allergen affects the entire family and every friend. The allergen affects school, the workplace, going to a ball game, to a movie or a sleep over. An allergen changes everything – life changes in a dramatic way.

Guests Who May Not Understand

I recall a guest who ordered Shrimp Scampi, but the server heard his mother say "I thought you were allergic to shrimp". The server engaged the guest, and made him aware that we would not be able to serve him the Shrimp Scampi, but would check with the chef for other options. The guest became irritated, and I was called to the dining room to speak with him. He stated that he had not had a reaction in over 20 years. The conversation was simple:

"How do you know you are no longer allergic?" I asked.

No good answer.

"Do you carry an Epi-pen?"

"Yes," he replied.

"When was the last time you changed it?"

"I have never changed it," he replied.

We did not serve the guest shrimp that night.

GUESTS' RIGHTS AND RESPONSIBILITIES

Bottom line: a guest with food allergies has a right to dine safely in your restaurant. So where do we start? "A guest with food allergies is not an inconvenience or an interruption of service." We must embrace allergens in the hospitality industry, we as management must raise our level of commitment and create the environment within the restaurant where behavior becomes more than "do what I say". Management must work hard to remove all of the excuses. Managing allergens is doable with the right attitude, commitment to ensuring that policy and procedures are worker friendly. We must strive to exceed industry best practices by providing advanced allergen awareness, advanced allergen knowledge and advanced training. This will ensure that each team member on all levels, and in every classification, while serving a food allergic guest will be able to answer questions, and provide reasonable accommodations accurately and with confidence.

I believe that a food allergic guest's responsibility is equal to, or greater than, the restaurant's responsibility. Once a restaurant is made aware of the allergen, the restaurant must be committed through training, policy and industry best practices to serve the food allergic guest safely. ALL food allergic guests, parents of, and friends of, have a greater responsibility to accurately volunteer all food related allergy information to their server, we should not have to ask!!

THE REWARDS

You may have many great customers returning for one reason or another – great service, food was amazing, server made the day, etc. But for a food allergic guest who has placed their life, the life of their child, the life of someone they love in your hands, it's quite different. When you safely serve a food allergic guest, you have written a song in their hearts that can never be erased, you have created a bond, a level of trust that words cannot convey.

They trust you, they call you friend, they look forward to the next visit, because it may be the only time they feel free. It may be the once or twice a month when the stress level is on time-out, where for the next hour or two their heart beats normal, they feel normal, they feel included, they feel safe. A one to two hour window where parents are worry-free, they are getting some alone time, so to speak. When our attitude changes, when our commitment is unwavering, and our knowledge and awareness are aligned, we embrace the food allergic guest not some of the time, not most of the time, but all of the time. We have created a heart centered culture, an environment, a safe place for our food allergic guests.

At the South Point Hotel in Las Vegas serving up to 12,000 meals daily, we have a very active and robust Allergen Program, headed up by Chef Keith Norman.

All employees are trained on how to help customers with any Allergy or dietary needs, the procedures and protocol's that are in place exceed current industry best practices, as the Executive Chef it gives me peace of mind knowing that we can provide reasonable accommodations safely for all our customers here at the South Point.

Christopher Johns H.G.T.

Executive Chef

South Point Hotel, Casino, and Spa

The first key is changing attitudes!! No one likes change, so getting leadership to buy into life threatening food allergies is difficult when they have no story, no face, and no real life experience to relate too, only percentages. The second key is commitment. Once you have broken through the "we have done this before" attitudes, and the "it's not that serious" attitudes and "isn't that policy a bit extreme" attitude then management becomes committed to the goal of Food Safety/Allergen Safety compliance, the management buy-in is critical to building an allergen aware culture. The last key is knowledge, the basics, that's where you start.

If you don't like something, change it.
If you can't change it, change your attitude.
Maya Angelou

TRAINING YOUR TEAM

Being Supportive and Confident

Embracing and understanding the fear of a guest with food allergies is important, understanding the consequences is more important. Management must always be supportive, and the team must feel in their souls that management has their backs. Training must be consistent and sustained because training is changing behavior. Training goes above and beyond policy and procedures, training is attitude, commitment, knowledge and executing policy and procedure with a positive attitude. We must commit to ensuring that all food allergic guests can dine safely and with confidence. It is important that we recognize that our guests have expectations, and they are trusting that you are allergen aware, knowledgeable and have basic training in serving someone with food allergies.

Patience

Training the team to handle guests with food allergies takes a lot of patience, but they need to see it in a positive way which is why the team must have input. We are asking them to do something different. Allow them to be a part of the process so that they own it, so it becomes more than just another thing they have to do. Training takes time, training must be consistent, sustained and evaluated often, because each guest presents different opportunities, and the guest with food allergies is your greatest teacher in most cases. Through training and awareness, the team must be prepared to embrace the risk taker "a little won't hurt me", and the newly diagnosed "we are not that knowledgeable but my son is allergic to..." as well as the "I am an adult and should be able to order what I want". Take a deep breath and trust your training!

CREATING AN ALLERGY TRAINING CULTURE, ENVIRONMENT AND ATTITUDE

Getting Executive Management On Board

Regardless of the restaurant, pub, bar, catering event or cafeteria, allergen awareness and allergen standards begin with those at the very top. I have been fortunate in my journey to build one of the best allergen programs, by following the advice from industry experts, being aware of current laws and implementing the industry's best practices. But the most critical element to all the effort was executive management. In all fairness some of my Executive Managers live with food allergies, so it was easier to get them on board. Yet the mission of convincing upper management that investing in allergen training, allergen certification and implementing allergen procedures is the right thing to do is well worth any resistance. Executive management will question whether an allergen program is necessary even when you reference current laws and current cases. Often you will have to fight through skepticism because upper management may not have all the facts, or they look at how the program will impact guests who may not have life threatening food allergies. It may be a battle until they read something, see something on the news, hear from a colleague or eat at a restaurant where the service team asks "Are there any allergens or dietary concerns that I should be aware of". That will be their "ah ha moment".

All layers of Management are different and each layer comes with challenges that the facilitator must embrace from the 'know it all', to the 'I've done this before', to the 'some timer', to the 'we're too busy', to the 'why should I go above and beyond', to 'they should just eat at home' attitudes. I can say from experience that it's tough and frustrating to create an allergen-aware culture. But once you break through the barriers, once you demonstrate to the 'know it all' that there's more to learn, the 'I've done it before' that there is a better way, the 'some timer' that one time might cost a life, to the 'we're too busy', that we can do it even when we are busy, and that it won't be an inconvenience. Soon attitudes will begin to soften, and hearts begin to change.

When you witness proper policies and procedures being followed in a consistent and sustained manner, positive outcomes will surely follow. During this time, you will witness a heart centered culture change, a paradigm shift, and that is one of the most rewarding feelings possible.

FABlogCon

Anyone can say "we've done it before" and that would be a true statement in many cases. But there are not a lot of chefs that would be willing to take on a conference where almost everyone in attendance has a life threatening food allergy. FABlogCon (Food Allergen Blogger Conference) was the first major allergen undertaking. FABlogCon brought together a group of  amazing advocates and expert educators with the goal of providing tools that would help families navigate a little easier through their allergen journey. In 2013 I was honored to quarterback the first FABlogCon by pulling together different departments, coordinating training and being the liaison between the organizers and the hotel.

Chef Keith Norman was and remains a pivotal part of the national Food Allergy Bloggers Conference, FABlogCon: The Blogger & Consumer Advocacy Conference for those Managing Food Allergies or Celiac Disease. When planning the first event it was paramount that we had a chef who understood food allergies and was passionate about great food and providing safe meals. We were bringing hundreds of people together who all managed various dietary restrictions, celiac disease, anaphylaxic food allergies. These were our friends and colleagues, the meals HAD to be safe. Chef Keith has continued to help ensure the success of our event helping with menu planning, and staff trainings. As a professional and as a friend, he has my utmost admiration and respect.

Jenny Sprague
Founder of FABlogCon

Top Mistakes

Top mistakes that restaurants often make when dealing with a food allergic guest is having the *"we have done it before"* attitude, *"we are too busy"* attitude, or not having guidelines in place to address food allergies. As I mentioned, training upper management on all levels is key, because this is where change in attitude and behavior must begin. Every allergen opportunity is a different snap shot, the environment may be different, and the team may be different. Though we may have handled a thousand food allergic guests, today may be different. Complacency, being over confident, the thousand guests with food allergies that you served in the past, etc., but maybe this time you don't have the same tools in place. Often managers that have been in the industry for years, lack the commitment to training – becoming complacent, which is an attitude that needs to change. They don't see the value in training or the consequences for lack of. Management on all levels must be 100% committed to make it work.

Training is influencing a change or continuation of an action or behavior."
—Ross Page, Brighton, United Kingdom

PUTTING THE PLAN IN PLACE

This goes beyond the basic guidelines, because every step you take you must consider the human factor. The Chef, Manager, Assistant Chef, Assistant Manager, the cook, the server, the pantry, the busser and the kitchen workers – their exposure and their experience. Will it be just another Standard Operating Procedure that will add to the million things they already have to do, or will they embrace it? Changing behavior, especially when talking about food safety and allergen awareness has to start with making it real. Real has to be more than if you don't follow the guideline then I will "write you up". In my experience you must first tug on the heart strings, and that plan must first start with all layers of management.

"leadership is the art of getting someone else to do something you want done because he wants to do it"
Dwight D. Eisenhower

The plan must start with training all levels of Management, giving them the opportunity to put themselves in the food allergic guests' shoes, not only from the point of eating out but also eating in. The guest with food allergies' journey begins way before they have the courage to give your restaurant a try. Their lives outside the restaurant is challenging as well. When I taught at the Art Institute I would give my students two projects. The goal behind the projects was to get them in the zone, to give them a deeper understanding of not only how food safety would affect their careers but allergens as well. I tried to instill in them that though food safety and allergen safety at times would be challenging, that being pro-active versus reactive is the best practice.

I first asked my students to eliminate the top eight allergens from their meals for a week. They could not have peanuts, tree nuts, dairy, eggs, shellfish, fish, soy, gluten or wheat for seven days. This also meant they would have to source and verify packaged items to ensure that they were not made in a facility that processed items containing or used shared equipment that processed food items that could have been cross-contacted. I wanted them to have the experience of a total life style change, even if it was only for seven days.

The second project I would have them do is to go to their favorite restaurant, or to my restaurant, with a specific allergen. The years I have spent at conventions and conferences has made me aware of the fear an allergen family goes through wondering how the restaurant team will react once made aware of an allergen. What I like to call *the face*. "It's a busy day, my station is full and now I have to deal with your special needs, I am too busy for this" face. This sends the wrong message to the guest with food allergies. So I asked my students to make notes of the experience, positive or negative, and then if this was not a mock assignment, how would you feel?

In my opinion, as future Food Directors, Chefs, etc., it is critical that you establish a connection. It is very similar to when you hear on the news that a motorcycle rider had been forced off the road, hit the guard rail and unfortunately was killed. Later in the day the story was on the news again, but this time her picture was included. That created a completely different feeling – before it was just a name, now it is a person.

"When you hear dry statistics, they don't mean anything until you attach a face, a story or a life to those statistics. Everyone of those statistics stand for a human being who had dreams, loves and passions"
Nancy Donnelly

Changing the Culture

The plan must begin with changing the culture, getting everyone to understand the importance of food safety and allergen awareness. And then giving your team the tools and a standard operating procedure. At this point it is important to evaluate each restaurant, especially if each menu is different, each team is different and certainly the way they execute service will be different. So you must look at how the changes will affect the flow. The goal is to keep the guest safe with minimal interruption to the flow, this is what I call the "coaching up" moments that give both the kitchen team and the service team confidence. For example, once everyone has been trained on food safety and allergen awareness, they will be able implement these steps every day, whether busy or slow. The attention and focus will be the same. Every guest with food allergies' life matters. The extra ten minutes to check ingredients, the extra ten steps to consult with the chef is not an inconvenience, it is a necessity.

Where to Start

Creating an allergen aware culture is not easy. In boot camp when a platoon is learning to march, the drill instructor will first demonstrate the steps. Then after at least a dozen tries, the group will start to move as one. The soldiers must practice for hours on one move until it was perfect; allergen awareness training must have the same commitment. Every level of management must be engaged and then every classification must be trained. Allergen awareness is not only for food and beverage departments, often bellmen, valet and departments that indirectly serve a guest with food allergies are overlooked.

Support Departments

Support departments must be part of the training and conversation. Bellmen, porters, kitchen workers, spa attendants and housekeepers must be trained. They must be included and made aware of the potential of cross-contact. Cross-contact is what happens when the allergen protein is transferred from one surface to another. Though this might be a non issue for normal businesses, when you host an allergen conference, there are multiple life threatening allergens in the group. So the banquet catering team puts together allergen friendly menus, all restaurants are alerted of the allergens and everyone is in allergen alert mode, yet the supporting departments are not in the loop. So let's look at the bell desk as an example. Mr. and Mrs. Jones and their daughter, Ashley, have spent an allergen episode free time at the amazing allergen conference. They are about to check out, and have asked the bell desk to pick up their bags from the room. Ashley, the daughter, is deathly allergen to peanuts. The bellman, who is sent to the room to pick up the bags, loves honey roasted peanuts, and has a jar at his station, and has been snacking on them over the course of his shift. He picks up the bags, brings them to valet and loads them in the Jones' car. Ashley remembers her laptop is in her bag, shortly after opening the bag, Ashley has a reaction.

So when it comes to allergen awareness it is not only about creating an allergen culture or embracing the journey, management must be forward thinkers, "it's not what you know, but what you should have known".

WHAT I HAVE LEARNED

Attitude

Over the years I have learned a lot from my allergen families. Attitude is key to embracing food allergic guests; a good friend once said that we have never met anyone that wanted to hurt our kids. Understanding that when preparing food items your behavior changes in relationship to business. When a restaurant is slow we can take more time and care in the preparation of a meal. When we are busy, we tend to speed up the process, not paying too much attention to detail. But when we are dealing with a guest with food allergies, our attitude must be the reverse, that is the time for focus and due diligence.

Commitment

Time builds commitment. It must be a constant reinforcement of why we are doing what we are doing. At first, most will not take allergens seriously – it's new, it's an inconvenience, what happens when I am busy, ugh another change, just one more thing I have to do, etc.

We make a commitment to continue to keep food allergic customers safe. Our customers will be safer, and we as individuals will be better for it.

Knowledge

Stick with the basics, do not overload, and be patient. Start with the top eight allergens, and build from there.

Every operation is different, what works for one restaurant may not work for another, so you must be patient, think about the ultimate goal – safely serving a food allergic guest. Then look at the flow in your restaurant, look at your "touch points" from first contact to the time the guest says good bye. Look at all the critical control points where cross-contact can occur, and add procedures that will address them. Every operation will come with it's own set of challenges. Training may not be the same for everyone, you must look at each food and beverage outlet, observe what happens, and then look at the areas that need to be addressed.

———————— TOP EIGHT FOOD ALLERGENS ————————

PEANUTS   TREE NUTS   COW'S MILK   EGGS

SHELLFISH   FISH   SOY PRODUCTS GLUTEN & WHEAT

WRITING A STANDARD OPERATING PROCEDURE (SOP)

A written Standard Operating Procedure (SOP) will allow you to maintain consistency and continuity throughout the food, beverage and supporting departments. Training and certification should be the first step. We must ensure that all levels of management, and all food and beverage classifications are knowledgeable and aware of the top eight allergens which account for 90% of reactions, as well as the derivatives and other common allergens. The SOP must include food allergies, intolerances and sensitivities as well as celiac disease.

Allergen Hazard Analysis

In the 1960's the Pillsbury Company was tasked to design a scientific based system to identify food safety hazards and steps needed to reduce or eliminate each hazard related to foodborne Illness for the NASA Program.

The Hazard Analysis Critical Control Point (HACCP) program addressed Biological, Chemical and Physical hazards. The HACCP program allows you to look at each step in the flow of food indicating where foodborne illnesses can occur, helping you implement measures to prevent illness or injury. This system can also be applied to allergen programs.

The Critical Control Point (CCP) Decision Tree was a very useful tool in creating my Allergen Program. A CCP is any point in the flow of food where steps must be taken to reduce or eliminate food hazards. The Decision Tree helps in identifying CCPs.

When creating your Allergen SOP, first look at the restaurant and kitchen as a whole, taking into consideration how food and beverages are currently being handled by both the service and culinary teams.

An Allergen Hazard Analysis is analyzing the flow of food, from the time the guest says "allergen" to the time the guest receives the meal. Looking at each step, identifying CCPs and puting steps in place to eliminate the allergen.

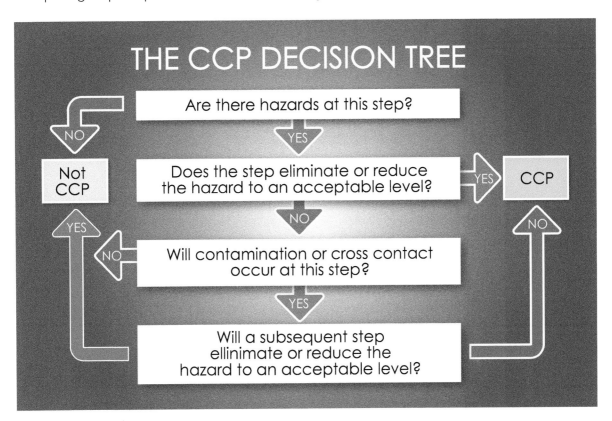

The following steps are only guidelines – you must evaluate your operation and implement an SOP that makes sense for your respective food and beverage operations. Consult your legal team, and include them in the planning process so you can get their input from the beginning. Your SOP is a working document which will change from time to time.

SOP for Handling Food Allergic Guests and Dietary Concerns

Let me stress that the SOP is a road map to serving your food allergic guests safely. Treat all allergies, sensitivities and intolerances the same – a mushroom or peanut allergy should be handled the same way as a sensitivity to pepper or an intolerance to dairy. When made aware of a food allergy, treat the guest that says their allergy is not that serious the exact same way you treat a guest who says their allergen is severe. Do not gamble, and as many experts will tell you, by saying no, you may lose a customer, but it is better to lose a customer than to risk someone's life.

1. All Room Managers, Room Chefs and Assistants are allergen aware and have received advanced training and certification. Refresher training must be conducted yearly.

2. Frontline Staff have received advanced allergen awareness training and certification. Refresher training should be conducted yearly.

3. Allergen Alert signs will be displayed at the entrance of each restaurant as a reminder for guests to inform the Server of any allergen or dietary concerns.

4. Menu notice to guests *"Please make your Server aware of any food allergies prior to ordering"* and a *"May contain..."* statement making the guest aware that menu items may contain peanuts, tree nuts, fish, shellfish, dairy, eggs, soy and/or wheat.

5. Allergen awareness posters listing common allergens and the derivatives, how to read a label, hidden ingredients, gluten and emergency procedures will be posted in all food prep areas in the kitchen.

6. Cross-contact is one of the biggest challenges for the kitchen, especially during peak business hours. Allergen tool kits (Allergen Saf-T-Zone System) will be made available in all kitchens to help avoid cross-contact.

7. Once the Server is made aware of a food allergy or dietary concern, he or she should immediately alert the Manager or Supervisor on duty.

8. Though the top eight allergens are the most common, the procedure is the same for all allergens, intolerances or sensitivities presented to you by the guest.

   - Once the special dietary restrictions (allergen(s)) are identified it will be written down by the Server using the Allergen Alert Pad and repeated back to the guest for accuracy. At this time the Server should ask if there are specific menu items that the guest is interested in, the Server should not make meal recommendations at this time but should take the information to the Chef or Kitchen Supervisor.

- The Chef or Kitchen Supervisor should evaluate each course and provide safe options for the guest.

- A guest may attempt to order around the allergen and may not make you aware. The service team must be aware of a guest that asks "Does this item contain xyz", "Can that be made without mushrooms", and "I will have the meatloaf no gravy." Any changes to normal menu items should prompt the server to ask the guest "Is there food allergies that I should be aware of?"

- The Chef or Kitchen Supervisor should evaluate each course (appetizer, salad, entrée and dessert) and provide safe options for the guest.

9. The Chef or Kitchen Supervisor should:
    - Review the menu items.
    - Review how to read a label poster.
    - Review the complete list of ingredients in the food items that are suggested.
    - Review with the Server the safe items that will be presented to the guest.

After safe options are reviewed with the Server and the Kitchen Supervisor, the Server should convey this information to the guest. Then the guest should be offered alternatives to the allergen, but they will not be served anything inclusive of the allergen mentioned.

For more information about training and certification, visit this website:
https://www.foodallergyawareness.org/education/restaurants%5Cdining_out-6/

For information about ANSI-accredited training and certification visit FAACT at:
https://www.foodallergyawareness.org/education/

Often a guest may not fully realize the severity of food allergies, intolerances or sensitivities and may demand that you give them what they have said they are allergic too. Refuse to do so, offering alternative options – trust your training and follow your SOP.

The Point of Sale System (POS)

All systems are similar, and can be programmed to include what items contain what allergens. This can help when placing orders and communicating with the kitchen staff. Here are the steps for the system I use.

Server will:

- Swipe card to open terminal

- Open check with table number and guest count

- Select food item

- Hit allergy alert (pop up of all allergens show)

- Select the allergy that the guest has made us aware of (example-fish-shellfish-milk). Keep in mind that a guest may say 'no tomatoes' but may simply dislike tomatoes, so it is a preference. Add a key (PREF) as this information still needs to be communicated with the kitchen.

- Send the order to the kitchen - Accurate information is critical to preparing the allergens guest's meal safely. Once the server has filled out the alert slip and consulted with the Chef it must be put into the POS system correctly.

- Verify that the check is received - Once the allergen check is received the Chef must make sure that the check matches the allergen alert slip.

When picking up the order the Server will:

- Speak directly to the Chef or Kitchen Supervisor to receive the allergen meal which will be identified with a purple allergen dot placed on the lid

- The Servers role is critical at this point, they must be absolutely sure that they are receiving the correct meal

Steps to food allergy safety once the order is received in the kitchen

Every kitchen is busy, every kitchen has its own unique challenges that make serving food allergic guests stressful but it is the attitude, the commitment, the proactive not reactive approach, that will ultimately allow you to serve your food allergic guest safely.

Excuses, work hard to remove all excuses:

- It's busy season...What's the plan?

- We are short staffed today...What's the plan?

- We are not sure we can safely serve a food allergic guest with multiple allergies... What's the plan?

Like an emergency evacuation or fire drill, you must have a plan in place, and it must be practiced daily until it becomes a habit.

- When the allergen meal request is received in the kitchen, the Chef or Kitchen Supervisor must prepare or directly supervise the preparation of the allergen meal on all stations.

- If the Chef or Kitchen Supervisor is not in the kitchen when a allergen order is received, they should be made aware immediately.

- The person preparing the meal must first wash their hands and put on allergen specific purple gloves which are dedicated to allergen meal preparation.

- All allergen meals will be prepared using the allergen saf-t-zone system (purple kit) provided in each kitchen – this will help prevent cross-contact while preparing the meal.

- All ingredients must be taken from a dedicated source, the mise en place on your line may have been cross-contacted during normal business use, for example the tongs used on a food line are often used to handle multiple ingredients.

- If during the preparation you make a mistake, you must start over. For example if the burger was no cheese and you added cheese do not try to remove the cheese, make a completely new burger. If the steak called for no sauce and sauce was added, do not try to scrape it off, make a new steak.

- When the allergen meal is completed, the Chef or Kitchen Supervisor must verify that this is the allergen meal, and immediately cover and place an allergen dot on the lid. The allergen meal should be given directly to the Server, or personally delivered to the guest by the Chef. Modify this step to support your current system if you do not use lids in your operation. I would recommend the last step of delivering the allergen meal be consistent – given directly to the Server or personally delivered to avoid cross-contact after preparation.

- To avoid cross-contact pre-wash and pre-label lids prior to service, do not reuse lids that have been used for other dishes.

- After using the allergen kit all items should be run through the dish washer and returned to the kit.

Buffet Standard Operating Procedures for Handling Food Allergic Guests

It is never recommended that a buffet be the first option. A production kitchen at a buffet can be quite busy, which means cross-contact can be a huge problem. Production workers are in "the zone" as they often support multiple food outlets. They are on strict schedules, and don't want to get yelled at if the Emice of Veal is not on the line in time? It is easy while cooking three or four different food items at one time to accidently add allergens to a dish without even noticing it, especially when production workers share equipment – pots and pans, utensils, etc. Therefore it's not uncommon to accidently add an ingredient to a sixty gallon kettle, not realizing it until it's too late. Mistakes like that happen in every kitchen setting, even at home. Also, the frontline is a common place where cross-contact can happen – from simply not changing gloves when handling different food items, using the same cutting board, oven, fryer or utensil. Sometimes guests will even use the same serving spoon for multiple dishes, thinking it will make the buffet line move faster, creating a cross-contamination nightmare in the process. Generally speaking, it is better to discourage a food allergic guest from eating at buffets.

Even with that being said, a guest can still dine safely in a buffet environment. We must be sensitive to food allergic guests who are on a budget, or just like the idea of variety in the same meal. Reasonable accommodations may appear different in a buffet environment verses a free standing restaurant, where items are made to order and not in bulk. Though this can present a different challenge, with forward thinking and a plan in place, you can accommodate a food allergen guest without interruption to the normal flow of business.

- Once the guest has made the buffet host or server aware of an allergy, the host or server will make the manager, supervisor and Chef on duty aware.

- The Chef on duty will walk the line with the guest and direct them towards the menu items that will be safe to eat. Most often a food allergic guest with one or two allergies can safely dine with some guidance – communication is key. The Chef will know the ingredients used in each dish, and how the items are prepared, including the multiple layers of ingredients. The choices may be somewhat limited, but in my experience a food allergic guest is not picky, they just want safe options.

- Make the guest aware that there is a possibility of cross-contact, which holds true for any kitchen. It may be necessary to prepare the guest's meal fresh, and not allow them to eat from the line at all. Once again, with forward thinking you are prepared. It may take some additional time, but the guest will appreciate you making them feel safe. And this will go a long way in building friendships and relationships with our food allergic guests.

- It is recommend that the entire meal be freshly made for any food allergic guest with more than two allergies.

Banquet/Catering Standard Procedures for Handling Food Allergic Guests

Chefs, Managers and Staff are knowledgeable and aware of not only the top eight allergens (peanuts, tree nuts, dairy, eggs, shellfish, fish, soy, gluten and wheat) including the derivatives and other common allergens.

This written standard operating procedure will allow us to maintain consistency and continuity throughout the Banquet/Catering Departments when preparing plated, buffet or catered special event food items.

Steps to Food Allergy Safety

1. At the time of booking, the catering representative will inquire as to whether or not any of the group attendees have food allergies. If so, a list of the guests and their allergies a minimum of 30 days prior to their event.

2. The allergy information will be distributed to the appropriate hotel department managers (Banquet Manager, Banquet Captain, Banquet Chef and Garde Manger) once received from the client.

3. Each Manager will be responsible for communicating this information to his/her staff. The Banquet Manager & Banquet Captain will get together with the Banquet Chef to decide on a meal suitable for each guest and discuss with the Banquet Lead Servers who will be in charge of serving meals to the guests with food allergies.

4. At the pre-meal meeting, the Banquet Captain and Lead Server(s) will outline the menu for the function and discuss special arrangements and food allergy meals:

   a. The guest is seated and advises server they have a food allergy and have requested a special meal

b. The server locates the lead server in the room

c. The lead server approaches the guest and verifies the guest name appears on his/her list and reconfirms the allergy

d. The lead server delivers the prepared meal for the guest

e. If the guest name does not appear on the list or if we are made aware of an allergen directly by a guest, the lead server confirms the allergy(ies)

f. The lead server finds the Banquet Captain. The Banquet Captain then talks to the Banquet Chef to decide what he/she has available to meet the guest's needs

g. The lead server delivers the meal to the guest.

Steps to Food Allergy Safety in the Kitchen

- The Banquet Chef or 2nd Cook must prepare or directly supervise the preparation of the allergen meal.

- The person preparing the meal must first remove their gloves, re-wash their hands and put on clean allergen specific purple gloves.

- The allergen kit should be used in the preparation of all meals to help prevent cross-contact

- Once the allergen dish is completed a clean lid with a purple allergen dot will be immediately placed on the dish.

- Allergen meals should be stored in a manner that will not cause cross-contact.

The Purple Allergen SAF-T-ZONE SYSTEM must be used when preparing food items during service for a guest with multiple allergens or preparing multiple ingredients.

After using the allergen kit all items should be run through the dish machine and returned to the kit.

Banquet and Catering ALLERGY LIST

Name	Initial	Meal	Notes	#
Maria	A	Chicken / Chicken	Food Allergies: Allergic To Gluten Must Be Gluten-Free	4
Tricia	E	Food Allergies/Religious Restrictions	Gluten Free Steak/Chicken Preference If Compatible	1
Sara	H	Steak / Chicken	Shellfish	5
Kimberly	J	Steak / Chicken	No Dairy (Cheese, Butter, Etc), Gluten (Bread, Wheat Flour, Etc), Or Corn (Corn Meal, Corn Syrup, Corn Bread, Etc).	6
Mayrubis	A	Steak / Chicken	Shellfish(Shrimp, Lobster, Crab)	5
Alex	A Jr.	Steak / Chicken	Allergic To Shellfish	5
Christopher	B	Food Allergies/Religious Restrictions	(Combo Plate Lc) No Shellfish/Shrimp	5
Dewayne	B	Steak / Chicken	No Carrots Or Starches. Double Veggies Is Requested Per Dietary Restrictions.	7
Terence	B	Steak / Chicken	Shell Fish	5
Stacey	B	Steak / Chicken	Dairy Allergy	6
Dominique	C	Food Allergies/Religious Restrictions	Gluten Free (LC) - Allergic To Wheat, Gluten, Modified Food Starch. Prefer Steak If Possible.	8
Shelby	F	Steak / Chicken	Gluten Allergy (Legit One)	1
Alexisa	H	Steak / Chicken	Shellfish Allergy	5
Jordan	J	Steak / Chicken	Nut, Dairy, Citrus	6
Raven	J	Steak / Chicken	Combo Plate (LC) Lactose & Acid Reflux	6
Jonathan	K	Vegetarian	No Mango	10
Angelique	L	Vegetarian	No Mango	10
Amanda	M	Steak / Chicken	Walnuts	5
Marie	O	Steak / Chicken	No Gluten Please	1
David	P	Steak / Chicken	All Nuts Seafood (Especially Shellfish) Sweet Potatoes/Yams	5
Jordan	P	Steak / Chicken	All Nuts & Seafood (Especially Shellfish) Sweet Potatoes/Yams	5
Michelle	R	Steak / Chicken	Highly Allergic To Capsaicin (Chili Powder)	9
Joshua	S	Steak / Chicken	Gluten Free (LC) - Meal Is Required	1
Jason	S	Steak / Chicken	No Pork/Pig/Ham/Bacon Products	5
Shana	S	Vegetarian	No Pork/Pig/Bacon/Ham Products.	10
Stephanie	T	Steak / Chicken	Gluten Free (LC)- Dairy, Nut And Gluten Allergies	6
Roshanda	T	Steak / Chicken	Shrimp Allergy	5
Justin	T	Steak / Chicken	Severely Allergic To Spinach And Bananas	5
Wilbert	W	Steak / Chicken	Peanut Allergy	5

1. Combo Dinner NO SAUCE Gluten Free
2. Double Beef
3. Double Chicken
4. Double Chicken NO MARINADE/NO SAUCE
5. Regular Combo Dinner
6. Combo NO SAUCE/RICE/STEAMED VEG/NO TOMATO
7. Combo NO SAUCE/DOUBLE BROCOLLINI
8. Double Beef NO SAUCE
9. Combo-NO PEPPER JUST SALT/STEAMED VEG/NO TOMATO
10. Vegan Dish

Catered Buffets and Special Events

As mentioned, a buffet can be very challenging for a food allergic guest, but with forward thinking it is doable. A buffet is much different from a plated dinner where there is more control. Every effort should be made at the time of booking to get allergen information, but being pro-active and anticipating possible issues will minimize the frustration with last minute requirements.

Best Practice for Buffet Events

Add the item description to the menu (Chicken Marsala: Lightly floured chicken breast, sautéed with garlic, shallots and deglazed with Marsala Wine). This procedure informs the guest of the ingredients. You can also include the ingredients in an item's description on the buffet line. Always make Management aware of any food allergies or dietary concerns.

Keep in mind that food allergic guests have a responsibility to make you aware of their food allergy or dietary restriction. Though they play a huge part in their own safety, they may not always communicate their allergy concerns. Make it easy for a food allergic guest to ask questions, a 'Please make us aware' sign is inviting – it tells the guest that you have the knowledge needed, are asking the guest to communicate their concerns, and that you have a plan in place, therefore they are not an inconvenience. We are all in this together.

Catered Special Events

Remember that food allergic guests may attend the big game, or other special event that you are hosting where comfort or concession style food will be served. Unlike a plated dinner or buffet, special (Super Bowl) type events are open to the public, therefore the attendees may not have access to the menu. It is good practice to display signs inviting the guest to communicate their allergy concerns. Add verbiage to menu boards or to the invitations. In some cases an announcement can be made before the start of the event. Be sure to plan ahead so there will be safe options and accommodations available, which may include the allergen guest bringing their own food.

As a Banquet Chef providing safe meals for my allergen guests has become a way of life. Is it challenging and frustrating at times, YES! But I am confident in the training that my team and I have gone through here at the South Point. A banquet kitchen in its own right is a hectic environment but when it comes to food allergies the Banquet Chef must be the calm voice in the room. It is important to be proactive and plan for allergens in every function. The rewards after safely serving an allergen guest are quite gratifying.

Respectfully,
Chef Jamie Poltrock
Banquet Chef, South Point Hotel, Casino and Spa

Café and Room Service Standard Operating Procedures (SOP) for Handling Food Allergic Guests

You must evaluate your café and room service operation. A café/coffee shop and room service environment in regards to food allergic guests will be more challenging. Our Café Servers and Room Service Cashiers are the first people to talk with a food allergic guest. Therefore knowledge, awareness and advanced training and certification is key.

1. Once a guest has made the cashier aware of a food allergy, the information is written down using the allergen alert slip (*page 90*).

2. The Chef on duty is notified and the allergen SOP is followed. Guest is made aware of safe options and the order is put into the POS system. The guest is not in front of you when ordering room service, therefore it is critical that the information is written down accurately and repeated back. The team member interacting with the guest may not be aware of the menu preparations, therefore communication is crucial.

Allergen Friendly Menus

Restaurants can use their existing menus and will use check marks or X's to identify what the food item is free of. A food allergic guest should still ask questions about how the meal will be prepared.

Sample Menu Check List

	Wheat	Soy	Milk	Egg	Fish	Shellfish	Tree Nuts	Peanuts	Corn	Sulfites	Sesame	Legume	Onion	Mushrooms
Vegetables	X	X	X	X		X			X	X		X	X	X
Edamame	X	X		X								X		
Tempura Vegetables	X	X	X	X	X	X			X		X	X	X	X
Spare Ribs	X	X	X	X	X	X			X	X	X	X	X	X
Green Beans	X	X		X					X	X		X	X	

Shrimp	X	X		X		X			X	X		X	X	
Chicken Lettuce Wraps	X	X			X			X		X	X	X	X
Vegetable Lettuce Wraps	X	X								X	X	X	X
Chinese Spare Ribs (6)	X	X	X	X		X			X		X	X	X	X

There are many things to consider when writing an allergen friendly menu. But having a solid HACCP based allergen SOP in place minimizes the risk of making mistakes.

When creating an allergen friendly menu, I suggest using the KIS method (keep it simple). Using your current menu, consider which dishes can have the top eight allergens removed, and have minimum preparation steps, and remember KIS.

Supporting Teams – Front Desk, Bell Desk, Valet, Spa and Housekeeping Awareness

Certification is not necessarily needed for the supporting teams – front desk, bellman, valet, spa or housekeeping, but it is helpful. Typically support staff members would not be aware of a guest with allergies unless the guest mentions it. The main point of having supporting teams allergen aware is to ensure that they are directed to someone who can answer the questions. For example, a valet attendant could be the first to have contact with a guest with allergies while taking their car, or opening a cab door as the guest arrives. Sometimes guests might ask if the hotel has allergen friendly restaurants? It is important that the valet knows that all of the restaurants are allergen friendly, and to let the guest know that they should make sure the restaurant managers are made aware of their allergies when they dine.

You must go a step further when hosting an allergen conference, because the supporting teams have contact with the guests and surfaces that the guest may touch.

As mentioned in Kim Hollinger's Story (page 23), Kendall had a reaction when her face came in contact with a fish tank at a hotel after a guest who had eaten peanuts touched it.

Expect the unexpected "Your responsibility to be ready for the fight never ends!"
James Yeager.

Allergen Procedure Summary

Every operation is different so you must take the time to evaluate each outlet from every possible touch point. From the point that the food allergic guest enters your establishment to the point where they leave you must look at the flow and consider everything. Get your staff involved – get their feedback and input. Remember that 90% of the time the service team is engaging the food allergic guest, so they have valuable first hand information.

Chef Norman, it was an honor to be under the tutelage of an amazing Chef! Thank you for all that you have passed onto me! God bless.
Gil Wolford

Leadership

Leadership must be the example for others to follow, with no buy-in from the top you will not get buy-in from the frontline management team or staff.

Employee participation

Employees are the frontline, consider their participation. Without them, safety plans are just ideas floating in space. Employees are the ones who live it every day. Without their dedication and participation, your food safety program has no chance of survival.

A commitment to training is a must – training doesn't cost it pays, when you are proactive and you invest before you have a situation you help to reduce costly liability.

Training helped me accommodate customers better, and give better customer service. It also helped in sharing more information with them.

Ammiel

Training gave me the very knowledge that I needed to be able to safely serve special needs guests like Kendall Hollinger.
The advanced training and certification has taken me to a whole new level of comfortable.

Denise

Training has helped establish a positive knowledge base while creating accountability. Training has created a trust between both teams and as we work together towards the common goal, it establishes good communication and helps the team provide great service.

Jason Monge

Training has brought awareness to my team about the seriousness of food allergies, and how it's not what you know but what you should have known that can impact our food allergic guests. Training has also helped us better understand what our food allergic guests go through on a daily basis. Advanced allergen training and certification has provided my team with the knowledge and skills necessary to safely serve food-allergic customers with confidence.

Vanya Lakic

Training gave us the knowledge to safely accommodate our food allergen guest comfortably. Knowledge is power. Treat all food allergies the same, as training has taught us that all allergies can be life threatening.

Coronado Café Team

ALLERGEN FREE MENU

Salad

Mixed Green Salad
cilantro oil with lemon and lime zest or oil and vinegar

Main Courses

Chicken Casa Blanca
broiled chicken breast served on a bed of sautéed spinach

Chicken Fajita
tender chicken breast sautéed with bell peppers, onions and tomato

Beef Fajita*
beef fajita sautéed with bell peppers, onions and tomatoes

Filet Mignon Al Champignon*
two 3 oz filet mignon broiled and topped with mushrooms and bell peppers

Dessert

Fresh Berries or Seasonal Fruit Cup

All Entrées Served with Fresh Vegetables

*Southern Nevada Health District Regulations governing the sanitation of food establishments 96.03.0800.2: "Thoroughly cooking foods of animal origin, such as eggs, fish, poultry or shellfish, reduces the risk of food bourne illness. Individuals with certain health conditions, may be at higher risk if these foods are consumed raw or undercooked.

Please Let Your Server Know If You Have Any Food Allergies or Dietary Restrictions

Years of training have given us the confidence to embrace our allergen guest, as we are reminded each year during refresher training, it's all about ATTITUDE!!!

Baja Miguel's Team

ALLERGEN FREE MENU

CORONADO CAFE

All entrées served with dinner salad with oil and vinegar or fresh squeezed lemon and lime

Salads

Orchard Salad
field greens, apple, orange slices, strawberries and dried cherries
with a raspberry vinaigrette

George's Salad
field greens, diced tomato, avocado, dried sweet cranberries and grilled chicken breast
tossed with red pepper vinaigrette

House Specials

Sautéed Chicken Breast with Asparagus
chicken breast marinated in fresh thyme, rosemary and olive oil

Roast Prime Rib of Beef*
with oil free baked potato (no Jus)

16oz. Porterhouse Steak*
with oil free baked potato

Desserts

Fresh Strawberries

*Southern Nevada Health District Regulations governing the sanitation of food establishments 96.03.0800.2: "Thoroughly cooking foods of animal origin, such as eggs, fish, poultry or shellfish, reduces the risk of food bourne illness. Individuals with certain health conditions, may be at higher risk if these foods are consumed raw or undercooked.

Please Let Your Server Know If You Have Any Food Allergies or Dietary Restrictions

The café is a fast paced atmosphere, and can be challenging when serving food allergic guests. Both the service and culinary teams must work together to ensure that the allergen is communicated accurately, and that food is prepared safely. We often assign one person per shift to handle all allergen meals. The training that my team and I have received over the years has been a game changer when preparing meals for our guests with allergies, sensitivities and intolerances.

Chef George Bailey
Coronado Café Room Chef

ALLERGEN FREE MENU

Appetizer & Salad
Baked Artichoke Hearts with Herbed Tomato

Sliced Tomatoes and Hearts of Palm with Herbed Lemon Oil

Main Courses
Gluten Free Ravioli
with kale and mozzarella cheese, served with a tomato basil sauce or soy butter with garlic and basil

Gluten Free Gnocchi
served with a tomato basil sauce or soy butter with garlic and basil

Sautéed Chicken Breast
with mushrooms, olive oil, salt and pepper

Roasted Chicken Breast
with basil oil, served with a medley of vegetable (carrot, zucchini and yellow squash)

8oz Filet
with sautéed mushroom and onions

Gluten Free Penne Pasta
served with vegetables and pomodoro sauce

Desserts
Gluten Free Flourless Chocolate Cake   Poached Pear

*Southern Nevada Health District Regulations governing the sanitation of food establishments 96.03.0800.2: *Thoroughly cooking foods of animal origin, such as eggs, fish, poultry or shellfish, reduces the risk of food bourne illness. Individuals with certain health conditions, may be at higher risk if these foods are consumed raw or undercooked.

Please Let Your Server Know If You Have Any Food Allergies or Dietary Restrictions

We all become more knowledgeable, aware and now take allergens very seriously. We are more confident when dealing with our guests and answering their questions.

Don Vito's Team

ALLERGEN FREE MENU

Primarily Prime Rib

All entrées served with baked potato and allergy free house salad served with fresh lemon or oil and vinegar

Roast Prime Rib of Beef
Served with fresh made beef jus

South Point Cut – our most popular cut, sliced thick for your pleasure

English – three thin slices for full enjoyment

Cowboy Cut – for the really hungry, extra thick cut with the bone

Entrées

Herb Rubbed Chicken Breast – tender chicken breast rubbed with fresh herbs
and oven baked, served with steamed vegetables

Mango Chicken – chicken breast topped with mango relish, served with steamed green beans

Medallions of Beef – filet medallions smothered in sautéed mushrooms

Filet and Chicken Duo – topped with sautéed mushrooms, onions and asparagus tips

Broiled New York Steak – 12oz center cut, cooked to your liking

Dessert

Warm Berry Compote, Baked Pears Topped with Cinnamon & Brown Sugar

Southern Nevada Health District Regulations governing the sanitation of food establishments 96.03.0800.2: "Thoroughly cooking foods of animal origin, such as eggs, fish, poultry or shellfish, reduces the risk of food bourne illness. Individuals with certain health conditions, may be at higher risk if these foods are consumed raw or undercooked.

Please Let Your Server Know If You Have Any Food Allergies or Dietary Restrictions

Allergen Awareness Training has been the differences in how we accommodate our allergen guests here at Primarily Prime Rib, with the right attitude, 100% commitment and knowledge we build trust.

Primarily Prime Rib

ALLERGEN FREE MENU

STEAK HOUSE

All entrées served with choice of baked potato, pressed potato or steamed asparagus

Appetizers

House Salad
mixed greens with cherry tomatoes, vinegar and olive oil dressing

Grilled Portobello Mushroom
marinated portobello mushroom grilled with asparagus and roasted red peppers, balsamic vinegar glaze

Entrées

Marinated Chicken Breast
chicken marinated in thyme, rosemary and pure olive oil, pan seared and flamed with sherry wine

Prime Rib Au Jus
dry aged prime rib, allergen free au jus and horseradish

Filet Mignon
charbroiled center cut tenderloin with sunflower café de paris butter

Lamb Chops Silverado
charbroiled Colorado lamb chops with mint demi sauce

Dessert

Fresh Assorted Berries

Southern Nevada Health District Regulations governing the sanitation of food establishments 96.03.0800.2: "Thoroughly cooking foods of animal origin, such as eggs, fish, poultry or shellfish, reduces the risk of food bourne illness. Individuals with certain health conditions, may be at higher risk if these foods are consumed raw or undercooked.

Please Let Your Server Know If You Have Any Food Allergies or Dietary Restrictions

Allergen Awareness Training has given us a clear understanding how to keep someone safe with food allergies, to make it work there needs to be a perfect mixture of compassion, professionalism and a SOLID standard operating procedure.

Humbly the Silverado Steak House Team

ALLERGEN FREE MENU

ASIAN RESTAURANT

Appetizer
Grilled Chicken Skewers or Grilled Beef Skewers
served on a bed of thinly sliced cabbage

Salad
Asian Chicken Salad
chicken breast, sweet cabbage, sweet orange & olive oil

Entrée
Pan Seared Chicken Breast or Chicken Thigh
served with steamed rice, steamed bok choy & baby carrots

Dessert
Fresh Cut Oranges

*Southern Nevada Health District Regulations governing the sanitation of food establishments 96.03.0800.2: "Thoroughly cooking foods of animal origin, such as eggs, fish, poultry or shellfish, reduces the risk of food bourne illness. Individuals with certain health conditions, may be at higher risk if these foods are consumed raw or undercooked."

Please Let Your Server Know If You Have Any Food Allergies or Dietary Restrictions

Food allergies have become more prevalent. Food allergies, dietary restrictions and preferences are increasing at an alarming rate.

Our training and certification helps us stay on the cutting edge, serving our food allergic guests is first and foremost for our raison d'etre is still all about the guest. Taking a moment of truth and turning it into a moment of trust is what gives us the most gratification here at Zenshin.

Humbly Submitted

Zenshin Restaurant Team

Training can only prepare you when you are given information. To all food allergic guests, your life matters, and we wholeheartedly want to give you the absolute best service in a comfortable environment – your safety is our priority.

Please remember that we get frustrated when guests:

- Do not take their food allergy seriously
- Say they are allergic when they are not
- Say they are allergic to shellfish, yet insist on ordering a shellfish dish
- Say they are not *that* allergic
- Say a little bit won't hurt them
- Say they can safely eat three shrimp, but any more will cause a reaction
- Say they've taken allergy medication before going out to eat
- Say they've brought their EPI-Pen
- Inform us they are allergic half way through their meal
- Insist on having what they've just told us they are allergic to
- Have someone else in their party order what they have just told us they are allergic to
- Tell us it will only cause mild discomfort
- Get angry at us for trusting our training and following our allergen protocol, which is put in place for their safety

Scenario – You be the Judge

A woman went to a restaurant with her 8 year old daughter. She told the cashier her daughter was allergic to milk. The cashier and manager promised to look at the book of ingredients and recommended she order the plain chicken sandwich, as it would be a safe choice.

The child ate a few bites of the sandwich and began feeling ill. The mother took her daughter home where she started having a major reaction. The mother injected her daughter with two epipens, but they didn't work.

The mother called 911 and then took her daughter to a nearby urgent care. Her condition worsened so she was taken by helicopter to a Boston trauma unit where she was sedated, intubated and spent the next three days in the ICU until she could breathe without machines.

The women went back to restaurant to inform the manager of the incident. After further investigation, it was discovered that the bread portion of the sandwich contained dairy (it was made with butter). Whether it was an oversight, or an accident, it was a devastating situation.

You be the judge:

☐ No fault of the restaurant

☐ Restaurant was careless

☐ Restaurant was negligent

☐ Not enough information undecided

Allergens – Tips for Restaurants

Each situation you encounter in your restaurant is unique. There is no "one size fits all" approach to any restaurant practice, including how to handle allergen issues. This is particularly true from the legal perspective where state laws and regulations, and local ordinances, can vary widely from place to place. That being said, below are some suggestions that I often pass along to my clients and others regarding allergens and food safety generally.[1]

1. **Safe ingredient storage and handling.** It starts at the beginning. Unsafe ingredient management is going to follow your food from preparation to your customers. All allergen-containing ingredients should be clearly and conspicuously tagged. It helps to use the common name of an allergen that is in an ingredient, so that it is easily recognized by anyone who sees it. A bright color should be used to tag allergen-containing ingredients, so they are readily observable by those hurrying through a kitchen. Allergen-containing ingredients should also be safely stored. If possible, store allergen-containing ingredients in a separate room or location to avoid cross-contact. If that is not feasible, more common-sense tactics should be employed, such as ensuring that ingredient containers are safely sealed, and not stacking allergen-containing ingredients on top of non-allergen ingredients.

2. **Separate area and tools.** Just like allergen-containing ingredients should be segregated in storage, they should be segregated once they are introduced into your kitchen. If a separate allergen-free work station is a possibility, that is a best practice. If not, the work station must be properly sanitized before an allergen-free item is prepared there. Allergen-free utensils should be used to prepare all allergen-free items. These should have bright colored handles so that everyone knows they are for allergen-free prep. If you can serve allergen free items on a specially marked plate (think a colored ring around the plate) this will let everyone know to be extra careful when they see that item coming through the kitchen. Allergen-free items should be served as soon as possible to avoid cross-contact.

3. **Training.** Like any other initiative, training is critical. I don't mean training just for the managers, or just for the head of kitchen. I mean training for everyone; from the front of house to the bussers. During a busy dinner service, any of these employees could be asked about allergen content, or notified that a diner has an allergy. Once an employee is on notice of an allergy, the entire restaurant is generally on notice for liability purposes, so all employees need to know what to do. They need to be prepared to execute the chain reaction, to make sure everyone involved in serving that customer (server, manager, chef, etc.) is aware of his/her allergy and act accordingly.

4. **Emergency medical devices.** Often, private restaurants are not required to keep emergency medical devices such as epinephrine or automated defibrillators on site. This does not necessarily mean that such devices shouldn't be kept on site, as they could mean the difference between life and death. If you are going to keep such devices in your restaurant, make sure your employees have training on how to administer them. Good Samaritan Laws in many states generally protect those undertaking life-saving efforts from liability. This protection may not apply where the user is reckless, therefore training on device administration is critical. Also, check your local laws. In some places, certain emergency medical devices are exempted from Good Samaritan Laws, meaning the general protections do not apply.

5. **Document your efforts.** Oftentimes, allergen disputes between restaurant and patron devolve into "he said, she said" scenarios, where a diner alleges something was not disclosed, and the server says otherwise. While these can be tricky issues to litigate, it helps when the restaurant has documented training that it puts its employees through on a regular basis. It also helps when the restaurant keeps track of how often each employee receives said training. For example, a server who says he disclosed the presence of an allergen to a customer, and can show that such a disclosure is consistent with the training he has received each of the last five years, can seem more credible to a jury than a server making a bare allegation.

6. **Review and update your training and procedures.** In today's world, the next best thing is here before we've mastered current technology. The same principle applies in your kitchens. As industry standards governing processes and procedures advance, and as federal, state, and local laws and regulations change, it is important to look at how those should be incorporated into your operation, and into your staff training. What made sense even a year or two ago may no longer be standard operating procedure. Besides laws and standards, it is important to update your ingredient lists any time there is a menu change, or modification in food preparation. If a sauce that didn't contain milk yesterday does contain milk today, employees need to know that before interacting with customers.

7. **Customer communication is critical.** If your restaurant is sued because a diner had an allergic reaction, a jury is most likely going to be asked if you took reasonable steps to protect your customers. To satisfy this duty, it is important that you establish good allergen communication with your customers. Menus listing ingredients (in common terms) is one way to disclose the presence of allergens. Another method is identifying dishes which contain a major allergen using icons or other means. Restaurants can also ask their patrons to disclose food allergies. This request can be made by a server at the time of ordering, or by a written request in the menu, on the front door, etc. Diners have a duty to take reasonable steps to protect themselves and observe warnings displayed.

8. **Double check insurance coverage exclusions.** Nobody wants a customer to get hurt in their restaurant, but at least if something happens you have insurance, right? Maybe not. Make sure you read your policy exclusions carefully. Is an allergic reaction an exacerbation of a preexisting condition, and therefore not a covered injury? If a patron has an allergic reaction after she leaves your restaurant, is there coverage even if the reaction was not "on site?" Is inadvertent cross-contact with an allergen an adulteration which is not covered? Do your best to make sure you understand the answers to these and other questions before a claim arises.

9. **Respond to allergic reactions in your restaurant.** If a customer has an allergic reaction while in your restaurant, get qualified medical assistance. Observe whether the customer has administered any medication, including epinephrine. Gather available records, including a list of all items ordered by that diner as well as those sharing his table (including drinks), a copy of the menu, and all available allergen notices. If appropriate, get statements from employees who interacted with the diner, including anyone who would have asked him about allergies or to whom he would have disclosed an allergy. Maintain all tickets, receipts, and surveillance. If possible, preserve the diner's food. At an appropriate time, meet with your employees to discuss and analyze what happened.

10. **Call your insurance carrier and/or attorney.** If you get notice that you are being sued, contact your insurance company as soon as reasonably possible. There are time limits to report claims, and litigation deadlines which must be met. Collect the records discussed above, including records of your food safety policies, records of employee training, and records of your investigation into the incident. If you have an attorney, this information should be forwarded to him/her so that your legal interests are protected.

Allergens – Tips for Consumers

Every dining experience can present unique challenges. If you or a family member has a food allergy, you know that your approach to dining may literally be the difference between life and death. While no one piece of advice can prevent every incident from occurring, below are some suggestions that I often pass along to consumers and advocacy groups regarding allergen safety in restaurants.

1. **Get educated.** It starts with knowing your, or your family member's, allergy. Ask yourself, what are the signs and symptoms of an allergic reaction? What ingredients can trigger an allergic reaction, and what are the various names of those ingredients that you may encounter when dining out? What should you do if a loved one is experiencing an allergic reaction? While there is some overlap between food allergies, each allergy is different. It's critical that you have the answers to these and other questions before dining out.

2. **Talk to your peers.** You're not alone! Peer groups are an incredible source of information and encouragement for those with food allergies. I often work with consumer/family support groups and those lobbying for legislative changes. These groups have important, practical tips for allergy sufferers, and the parents and spouses of allergy sufferers. These are the people that are going to know which local restaurants have the best allergen controls and allergen-free options, which local doctors do the best job treating allergens, how to communicate with your children's

schools about food allergies, etc. This is often a free resource, and one where you can join-in and share your own experiences as well.

3. **Be prepared.** It's not just the Boy Scout motto; it's good advice for those with food allergies as well. Being prepared encompasses keeping yourself, or a loved one, out of situations where an allergic reaction is likely to happen, and knowing what to do if you, or a family member, are having an allergic reaction. Among other things you should make sure you understand which menu options are allergen free and what the ingredients in each dish are. When dining out, you should always have allergy medication with you in case you encounter unexpected circumstances. Best practice is to have at least two epinephrine injectors with you so that you have a backup in an emergency.

4. **Review available information.** Generally, restaurants have a duty to keep their customers reasonably safe. Diners have a reciprocal duty to act reasonably and observe warnings and other information which is there to be seen. It is important that you read the menu each time you dine, even if you've dined in the same establishment before, and ordered the same dish. Recipes, ingredients, and preparation techniques change. Nowadays, many menus list the ingredients in each dish. Others disclose allergens or use icons to denote the presence of an allergen (think of the image of a prawn to indicate an item contains shellfish). Make sure you have read and understood the menu information. Also, if your menu encourages you to notify your server of food allergies, do it. Oftentimes, restaurants will take extra care to protect patrons that they know have a food allergy, and that does not always happen merely because a customer orders a dish that is allergen-free.

5. **Ask.** You should always notify your server of a food allergy, whether or not a menu indicator or other placard requests that you do so. When you are ordering a dish – after you have notified your server of your allergy – ask to confirm that the dish does not contain the offending allergen(s). If the server seems unsure, ask him/her to check

with the kitchen. If another employee brings the meal to your table, ask that employee if the allergen is present and to double-check if he/she is unsure. While perhaps not legally required, these redundant inquires can help protect you from inadvertently consuming an ingredient which could trigger an allergic reaction.

6. **Be observant.** Anyone who has dined out with any regularity knows when a restaurant is busy. The lobby and bar are full of people, the tables are packed, and restaurant employees are moving at a feverish pace. Busy lunch and dinner rushes are the most likely times you will be dining out, and these are also the most likely times for an incident to occur. Where cooks and servers are hurriedly rushing from table to table and dish to dish, the likelihood of a mistake in food preparation or service is amplified. While some mistakes may be obvious (being served the wrong dish, breaded chicken which should be "naked," etc.) others are subtler (milk instead of juice in an opaque children's cup). Be as observant as you can, and trust your gut: if something doesn't look right, ask before consuming or serving to your family.

7. **Get appropriate medical attention.** The most important tip is to protect your health. If you are having an allergic reaction, administer the emergency medication which you brought with you to the restaurant immediately. If the restaurant calls an ambulance, get checked out by the EMT and follow his/her directions. If appropriate, follow-up with another medical provider or your own physician. Don't be embarrassed about your allergy or your reaction. Timing is critical, and a delay in treatment could mean the difference between life and death.

8. **Gather available information.** First, make sure that your health and safety, or that of your loved one, is secure. Once that is complete, gather available information about what happened. Collect as much information as you can about not only what you consumed, but also what was served to those at your table. Make a note of the names of the employees with whom you interacted, particularly if you notified them of your allergy, or if they told you that a dish was allergen-free. If the

restaurant wants you to make a statement and you are unable to do so, tell the restaurant you are unable to do so at this time. If you do make a statement, ask to be provided with a copy of it. If some of your food is remaining, ask to take a sample or have the restaurant preserve it. If the restaurant has surveillance or gets the identities of witnesses, ask that the information be passed on to you. While this is not a finite list, it is some of the information which may be available at the time an allergic reaction occurs.

9. **Consult an attorney if you are thinking about pursuing a claim.** An attorney experienced in dealing with food allergies should be able to guide you through the analysis of whether a legal claim worth pursuing exists. Ordinarily, initial consultations are complimentary, and a good opportunity for you to get answers to any questions you may have. Exploring your legal options does not mean that you have to file a lawsuit.

10. **Don't be afraid to follow-up with the restaurant.** If you have hired an attorney to represent you, or if you are thinking of hiring an attorney, that attorney should be the one communicating with the restaurant about your incident. If you have an attorney and the restaurant contacts you to discuss the incident, you may wish to direct the restaurant to your lawyer. But let's assume that you didn't hire an attorney, and you're not interested in pursuing a legal claim. You can still follow-up with the restaurant. Oftentimes, restaurant managers provide their contact information to those suffering allergic reactions. This is an opportunity for you to ask any questions you may have, or request the information identified above.

LABELS AND TOOLS

Allergen Dot
To be placed on lids of
allergen meals

Allergen Free

❏ No Dairy	❏ No Peanuts	❏ Gluten-Free
❏ No Eggs	❏ No Shellfish	❏ No Corn
❏ No Soy	❏ No Fish	❏ No Sesame Seed
❏ No Tree Nuts	❏ No Wheat	❏ Other_____

Allergen Free Label
To be placed on allergen free pots and pans

5 Piece Allergen Kit
To be placed in every kitchen,
with every staff member being
aware of its location

ALLERGEN ALERT

Server

Table #_____

Peanut	☐	Onion	☐
Tree Nut	☐	Garlic	☐
Fish	☐	Tomato	☐
Shell Fish	☐	Peppers	☐
Dairy	☐	Gluten	☐
Eggs	☐	Corn	☐
Soy	☐	Seasame	☐
Wheat	☐		

Other Instructions: _____
_____
_____
_____
_____

Allergen Alert Pad

To be used by food servers to communicate with kitchen staff

Buffet Sign

To be placed at the entry areas of all buffets

Allergen Alert

To Our Valued Guests

To help ensure that your dining experience is a safe and pleasant one:

Please be aware that milk, eggs, fish, shellfish, peanuts, tree nuts, wheat and soy may be present in food items served on the Buffet.

———

Please inform your server of **ANY ALLERGEN** or **DIETARY CONCERNS** and ask to speak with the Chef, Chef on Duty or the Restaurant Manager.

Thank You

Food Allergy – How to read a label

- Food allergy-related reactions account for over 30,000 emergency room visits and 200 deaths a year. Our Guests rely on accurate information about ingredients.
- This chart has been provided to give you the basic understanding of how to assist a guest with allergies. Please familiarize yourself with this information and refer to it each time you have a guest who has identified that they have an allergy.
- Education, cooperation and teamwork are key to safely serving a guest with allergies.
- Remember! A food allergy can be **DEADLY** if you are not 100% sure about the ingredients in an item, say so!!! And then call your Manager or Chef to answer guest's questions.

HOW TO READ A LABEL for a MILK-FREE DIET

Avoid foods that contain milk or any of these ingredients:
artificial butter flavor
butter, butter fat, butter oil
buttermilk
casein *(casein hydrolysate)*
caseinates *(in all forms)*
cheese
cream
cottage cheese
curds
custard
ghee
half & half
lactalbumin, lactalbumin phosphate
lactoferrin
lactulose
milk *(in all forms including condensed, derivative, dry, evaporated, goat's milk and milk from other animals, low-fat, malted, milkfat, non-fat, powder, protein, skimmed, solids, whole)*
nisin
nougat
pudding
recaldent
rennet casein
sour cream, sour cream solids
sour milk solids
whey *(in all forms)*
yogurt

May indicate the presence of milk protein:
caramel candies
chocolate
flavorings *(including natural and artificial)*
high protein flour
lactic acid starter culture
lactose
luncheon meat, hot dogs, sausages
margarine
non-dairy products

HOW TO READ A LABEL for a WHEAT-FREE DIET

Avoid foods that contain wheat or any of these ingredients:
bran
bread crumbs
bulgur
club wheat
couscous
cracker meal
durum
einkorn
emmer
farina
flour *(all purpose, bread, cake, durum, enriched, graham, high gluten, high protein, instant, pastry, self rising, soft wheat, steel ground, stone ground, whole wheat)*
gluten
kamut
matzoh, matzoh meal *(also spelled as matzo)*
pasta
seitan
semolina
spelt
triticale
vital gluten
wheat *(bran, germ, gluten, malt, sprouts)*
wheat grass
whole wheat berries

May indicate the presence of wheat protein:
flavoring *(including natural and artificial)*
hydrolyzed protein
soy sauce
starch *(gelatinized starch, modified starch, modified food starch, vegetable starch, wheat starch)*
surimi

HOW TO READ A LABEL for a SOY-FREE DIET

Avoid foods that contain soy or any of these ingredients:
edamame
hydrolyzed soy protein
miso
natto
shoyu sauce
soy *(soy albumin, soy fiber, soy flour, soy grits, soy milk, soy nuts, soy sprouts)*
soya
soybean *(curd, granules)*
soy protein *(concentrate, isolate)*
soy sauce
Tamari
Tempeh
textured vegetable protein (TVP)
tofu

May indicate the presence of soy protein:
Asian cuisine
flavoring *(including natural and artificial)*
vegetable broth
vegetable gum
vegetable starch

- Studies show most individuals allergic to soy may safely eat soybean oil.
- Most individuals allergic to soy can safely eat soy lecithin.

Check with your doctor if you have questions about these ingredients.

HOW TO READ A LABEL for a PEANUT-FREE DIET

Avoid foods that contain peanuts or any of these ingredients:
artificial nuts
beer nuts
cold pressed, expelled, or extruded peanut oil
goobers
ground nuts
mixed nuts
monkey nuts
nutmeat
nut pieces
peanut
peanut butter
peanut flour

May indicate the presence of peanut protein:
African, Asian *(especially Chinese, Indian, Indonesian, Thai, and Vietnamese)*, and Mexican dishes
baked goods *(pastries, cookies, etc.)*
candy *(including chocolate candy)*
chili
egg rolls
enchilada sauce
flavoring *(including natural and artificial)*
marzipan
mole sauce
nougat

- Mandelonas are peanuts soaked in almond flavoring.
- Studies show most allergic individuals can safely eat peanut oil (*not* cold pressed, expelled, or extruded peanut oil).
- Arachis oil is peanut oil.
- Experts advise patients allergic to peanuts to avoid tree nuts as well.
- A study showed that unlike other legumes, there is a strong possibility of cross reaction between peanuts and lupine.
- Sunflower seeds are often produced on equipment shared with peanuts.

HOW TO READ A LABEL for a SHELLFISH-FREE DIET

Avoid foods that contain shellfish or any of these ingredients:
abalone
clams *(cherrystone, littleneck, pismo, quahog)*
cockle *(periwinkle, sea urchin)*
crab
crawfish *(crayfish, ecrevisse)*
lobster *(langouste, langoustine, scampo, coral, tomalley)*
mollusks
mussels
octopus
oysters
prawns
scallops
shrimp *(crevette)*
snails *(escargot)*
squid *(calamari)*

May indicate the presence of shellfish protein:
bouillabaisse
cuttlefish ink
fish stock
flavoring *(including natural and artificial)*
seafood flavoring *(such as crab or clam extract)*
surimi

Keep the following in mind:
- Any food served in a seafood restaurant may be cross contaminated with fish or shellfish.
- For some individuals, a reaction may occur from cooking odors or from handling fish or shellfish.
- Always carry medications and use them as soon as symptoms develop.

HOW TO READ A LABEL for a TREE NUT-FREE DIET

Avoid foods that contain nuts or any of these ingredients:
almonds
artificial nuts
beech nut
Brazil nuts
butternut
caponata
cashews
chestnuts
chinquapin
coconut
filberts/hazelnuts
gianduja *(a nut mixture found in some chocolate)*
ginko nut
hickory nuts
lichee/lychee nut
macadamia nuts
marzipan/almond paste
nan-gai nuts
natural nut extract *(i.e., almond, walnut)*
nougat
nut butters *(i.e., cashew butter)*
nut meal
nutmeat
nut oil
nut paste *(i.e., almond paste)*
nut pieces
pecans *(Mashuga Nuts®)*
pesto
pili nut
pine nuts *(also referred to as Indian, piñon, pinyon, pignoli, pigñolia, and pignon nuts)*
pistachios
praline
shea nut
walnuts

- Mandelonas are peanuts soaked in almond flavoring.
- Mortadella may contain pistachios.
- Natural and artificial flavoring may contain tree nuts.
- Experts advise patients allergic to tree nuts avoid peanuts as well.
- Talk to your doctor if you find other nuts not listed here.

HOW TO READ A LABEL for an EGG-FREE DIET

Avoid foods that contain eggs or any of these ingredients:
albumin *(also spelled as albumen)*
egg *(dried, powdered, solids, white, yolk)*
eggnog
lysozyme
mayonnaise
meringue *(meringue powder)*
surimi

May indicate the presence of egg protein:
flavoring *(including natural and artificial)*
lecithin
macaroni
marzipan
marshmallows
nougat
pasta

© 2008 The Food Allergy & Anaphylaxis Network

Take Action
to Prevent an Allergic Reaction

Know the Most Common Food Allergens

Just think...

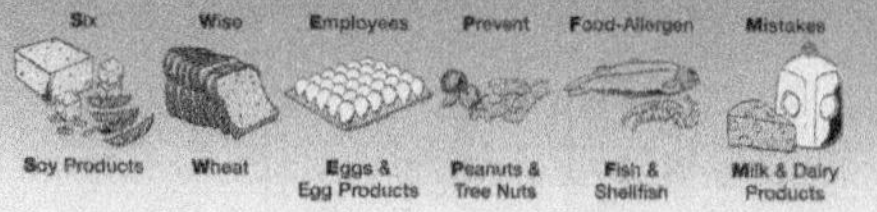

Avoiding Cross-Contact

To avoid cross-contact: wash, rinse and sanitize all utensils before each use, wash hands and change gloves before prep, and use separate equipment for customers with food allergies.

When Mistakes Happen

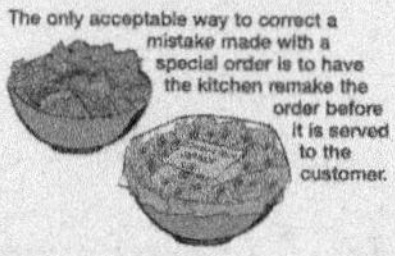

The only acceptable way to correct a mistake made with a special order is to have the kitchen remake the order before it is served to the customer.

Communicating with the Customer

Careful and effective communication with the customer and kitchen staff is the best way to protect the customer. Avoid a life-threatening situation by accurately describing dishes, identifying ingredients, and suggesting simpler menu items.

Symptoms of an Allergic Reaction

If a customer is showing symptoms of an allergic reaction, you must call 911 or your local emergency number, stay with the customer until help arrives, and then complete an incident report.

SYSCO ECOLAB CINTAS

National Food Safety Education Month®

HIDDEN ALLERGENS IN FOODS

LABELS THAT MAY INDICATE THE PRESENCE OF EGG PROTEIN

Albumin
Binder
Coagulant
Egg white
Egg yolk or yellow
Emulsifier
Globulin
Lecithin
Livetin
Lysozyme
Ovalbumin
Ovamucin
Ovamucoid
Ovovitellin
Powdered egg
Vitellin
Whole egg

FOODS THAT MAY CONTAIN EGG PROTEIN

Baked goods (most except some breads)
Baking mixes
Batters
Bearnaise sauce
Bouillon (in restaurants to clear it)
Breakfast cereals
Cake flours
Candy (see Sweets)
Cookies
Creamy fillings
Custard
Egg noodles
Eggnog
French toast
Hollandaise sauce
Ice cream
Lemon curd
Macaroni
Malted cocoa drinks (e.g., Ovaltine, Ovamalt)
Marshmallows
Mayonnaise
Meringues
Muffins
Noodles (egg)
Omelettes
Pancakes
Processed meat products (e.g., bologna, meat loaf, meatballs, sausages)
Puddings
Salad dressing (creamy)
Sherbets
Souffles
Soups
Spaghetti
Sweets (e.g., fondant creams, truffles, marshmallows, etc.)
Tartar sauce
Turkish Delight
Waffles
Wines (if cleared with egg white)

FOODS THAT MAY CONTAIN EGG PROTEIN

Batter-fried foods
Biscuits
Bread
Breakfast cereals
Cakes
Chocolate
Cookies
Cream sauces
Cream soups
Custard
Fish in batter
Gravies and gravy mixes
Ice cream (and "non-milk" fat)
Imitation sour cream
Instant mashed potatoes
Margarine
Muesli
Muffins
Other baked goods
Packaged soups
Pies
Puddings
Rusks
Sausages
Sherbet
Soy cheese
Soup mixes
Sweets
Canned soups
Vegetarian cheese

LABELS THAT MAY INDICATE THE PRESENCE OF MILK PROTEIN

Artificial butter flavor
Butter
Butter fat
Buttermilk solids
Caramel color
Caramel flavoring
Casein
Caseinate
Cheese
Cream Curds
"De-lactosed" whey
Demineralized whey
Dried milk
Dry milk solids
Fully cream milk powder
High protein flavor
Lactalbumin
Lactalbumin phosphate
Lactose
Milk
Milk derivate
Milk protein
Milk solids
Natural flavoring
Pasteurized milk
Rennet casein
Skim milk powder
Solids
Sour cream (or solids)
Sour milk solids
Whey
Whey powder
Whey protein concentrate
Yogurt

LABELS THAT MAY INDICATE THE PRESENCE OF SOY PROTEIN

Gum arabic
Bulking agent
Carob
Emulsifier
Guar gum
Hydrolyzed vegetable protein (HVP)
Lecithin*
Miso
MSG (Monosodium glutamate)
Protein
Protein extender
Soy Flour
Soy nuts
Soy panthenol
Soy protein
Soy protein isolate or concentrate
Soy sauce
Soybean
Soybean oil
Stabilizer
Starch
Textured vegetable protein (TVP)
Thickener
Tofu
Vegetable broth
Vegetable gum
Vegetable starch

MEMBERS OF LEGUME FAMILY

Beans
Aduki beans
Broad bean
Black turtle bean
Black-eyed bean
Chick pea
Cowpea
Fava bean
Garbanzo bean
Great Northern bean
Green bean
Kidney bean
Lima bean
Mung bean
Navy bean
Pinto bean
Snap bean
String bean
Wax bean

Other members
Alfalfa (sprouts)
Acacia (gum)
Carob (chocolate substitute)
Cassia or senna (in laxatives, curry, cinnamon)
Fenugreek (used in curries, cinnamon, primary flavoring in imitation maple syrup)
Lentils
Masur bean
Licorice
Pea
Green pea
Purple-hull pea
Peanut
Senna or cassia (in laxatives and Epsom salts)
Soybean
Tamarind
Tragacanth (gum)

LABELS THAT MAY INDICATE THE PRESENCE OF WHEAT PROTEIN

All-purpose flour
Bleached flour
Bulgur (cracked wheat)
Bran
Cornstarch
Couscous
Durum wheat
Enriched flour
Farina
Gelatinized starch* (or pre-gelatinized)
Gluten
Graham flour
Hard durum flour
High gluten flour
High protein flour
Hydrolyzed vegetable protein
Kamut
Miller's bran
Modified food starch*
Modified starch*
MSG** (monosodium glutamate)
Protein
Semolina
Spelt
Starch*
Unbleached flour
Vegetable gum*
Vegetable starch*
Vital gluten
Wheat bran
Wheat flour
Wheat germ
Wheat gluten
Wheat starch
White flour
Whole wheat
Whole wheat flour

FOODS THAT MAY CONTAIN WHEAT

Alcoholic beverages (made from grain alcohol)
Ale
Beer
Wine
Bourbon
Whiskey
Baked goods
Biscuits Breads (including rye bread)
Cakes
Cookies
Crackers, etc.
Baking mixes
Barley bread and drinks
Battered foods
Bouillon cubes
Breaded meats
Breaded vegetables
Breakfast cereals
Candy or chocolate candy
Canned processed meat
Cereal grains
Couscous
Gravy
Hot dogs
Ice cream
Ice cream cones
Luncheon meats
Licorice
Macaroni
Malt
Malted milks (e.g., Horlicks)
Milk shakes
Noodle products
Pasta (noodles, spaghetti, macaroni)
Pepper (compound or powdered flour filler)
Pies
Processed meats
Sausage
Semolina
Snack foods
Spaghetti
Soup mixes
Soups
Soy sauce
Tablets

FOODS THAT MAY CONTAIN PEANUT OR PEANUT OIL

Baked goods
Baking mixes
Battered foods
Biscuits
Breakfast cereals
Candy
Cereal-based products
Chili
Chinese dishes
Cookies
Egg rolls
Ice cream
Margarine
Marzipan
Milk formula
Pastry
Peanut butter
Satay sauce and dishes
Soups
Sweets
Thai dishes
Vegetable fat
Vegetable oil

LABELS THAT MAY INDICATE THE PRESENCE OF PEANUT PROTEIN

Ground-nut
Peanut
Peanut butter
Emulsifier (uncommon)
Flavoring
Oriental sauce

Take A Minute- Save A Life:

You Need To Know About Food Allergies

- ▶ Food allergies can kill
- ▶ Millions have food allergies
- ▶ Food allergies are on the rise in children
- ▶ There is NO cure for food allergies
- ▶ Staying away from food allergens is the ONLY way to avoid reactions
- ▶ When in doubt, tell the guest YOU DON'T KNOW

Any food can be an Allergen!

The most common food allergens are:

- Tree Nuts & Peanuts
- Milk Products
- Soy
- Wheat
- Fish & Shellfish
- Eggs

Spot A Reaction - Save A Life!

- ▶ Symptoms appear within seconds to hours
- ▶ Symptoms range from skin rash, to trouble breathing, to death
- ▶ Get help right away – **CALL SOUTH POINT SECURITY** #77550 or 0 - FOR THE OPERATOR

Food Allergies

It's A Matter Of Life Or Death

▶ MILLIONS HAVE FOOD ALLERGIES ▶ THE NUMBERS ARE GROWING
▶ TINY AMOUNTS OF FOOD ALLERGENS CAN KILL

EVERY FOOD HANDLER CAN SAVE A LIFE!

1 Take Customer Requests Seriously

- ▶ Listen Carefully
- ▶ Tell the chef about the food allergy
- ▶ Report back to customers how you can meet their needs

2 Check for Allergens Every Time

- ▶ Check recipes and food labels – food products may change
- ▶ Beware of allergens hiding in foods like sauces, soups dressings and oils

3 Stop Cross Contact

- ▶ Keep orders allergen-free from start to finish
- ▶ Start fresh – clean hands, gloves, workspace, utensils, pans and dishes
- ▶ Double check orders before serving – serve only if allergen free

Any food can be an Allergen!

Spot A Reaction

- ▶ Symptoms appear within seconds to hours
- ▶ Symptoms range from skin rash, to trouble breathing, to death

Save A Life!

CALL 911 (emergency)
if a customer is in distress

- ▶ Tell Management
- ▶ Stay with customer until help arrives

LABEL READING 1-2-3

INGREDIENTS:

SUGAR, UNBLEACHED AND BLEACHED ENRICHED FLOUR [WHEAT FLOUR, NIACIN, REDUCED IRON, THIAMINE MONONITRATE (VITAMIN B1), RIBOFLAVIN (VITAMIN B2), FOLIC ACID], CANOLA AND/OR PALM KERNEL OIL, HIGH FRUCTOSE CORN SYRUP, WHEY (MILK), FRUCTOSE, DEXTROSE, CORNSTARCH, EGG WHITES, SALT, CORN SYRUP, EMULSIFIERS (VEGETABLE MONOGLYCERIDES, SOY LECITHIN), LEAVENING (BAKING SODA AND/OR SODIUM ACID PYROPHOSPHATE AND/OR CALCIUM PHOSPHATE), EGGS, CORN FLOUR, NATURAL FLAVOR AND ARTIFICIAL FLAVOR, CARAMEL COLOR, SPICES.

CONTAINS: WHEAT, MILK, EGG, SOY.

MANUFACTURED ON EQUIPMENT THAT PROCESSES PEANUT, AND TREE NUTS.

Step 1

Look for a **"contains"** statement at the bottom of the ingredient list. If present, check to see if your allergen is listed. If listed, the item is **not safe**.

Step 2

Look for an advisory statement such as: **"may contain…,"** or **"processed in a plant…"** If present, check to see if your allergen is listed. If listed, it is recommended that you **avoid** this product.

Advisory statements are not required nor regulated. If there is no statement, you still may need to contact the manufacturer to find out their labeling practices for cross-contact and/or to ask if allergens are present in the manufacturing process.

If your allergen is not present in Steps 1 and 2, proceed to Step 3

Step 3

Read each ingredient on the ingredient label for the presence of your allergen. The allergen MUST be listed either in a "contains" statement OR in the ingredient list (not both). If your allergen is listed, the food is not safe to consume.

*The Food Allergen Labeling and Consumer Protection Act (FALCPA) only applies to FDA-regulated foods and only for the following allergens: **milk, egg, wheat, soy, fish, crustacean shellfish, peanuts, and tree nuts.** Allergens that are not covered by FALCPA do NOT need to be labeled and can be hidden in words such as: flavor, color, additives, or spices. If you are allergic to foods not covered by FALCPA, or are purchasing foods that are not FDA-regulated, you may need to contact the manufacturer for additional information.*

Written by Gina Mennett Lee, M.Ed.

I have learned over the years that a food allergic guest does not care about fancy, they care about safe. Because of this, when putting recipes together you must keep that in mind. As Master Chef Auguste Escoffier said "above all, keep it simple."

Early in my career at the Art Institute I taught a class called the Art of Cooking. The students were chefs from other Art Institute campuses around the country. After receiving and reviewing the syllabus I knew we were in for a fun class. So I put together my lesson plan, purchased a bag of Starburst candy, which is a good way to put the class into teams. Every chef would pull a Starburst candy out of a brown paper bag, and the matching colors would be their team. This technique takes students out of their comfort zone, and encourages them to mix and mingle.

After brief introductions the chefs split into their teams. We then reviewed the goals, expectations, course competency objectives and time frame needed to complete a three course meal. I then shared the kicker, which for seasoned chefs was the "Shut the front door" moment. They could use any fruits, fruit like vegetables, vegetables, starch and protein. But the only spices that could be used were salt and pepper. They did have a variety of salts and peppers they could choose from.

I am sharing a few simple allergen friendly recipes, but simple does not mean flavorless. Growing up in my grandmother's kitchen there were very few options for herbs and spices, yet salt, pepper, onions, garlic, sweet peppers, celery, carrots and an occasional big toe always seemed to do the trick. My inspiration for some of these recipes comes from my upbringing. Being on welfare meant leftovers, which is why my brother and I learned from my grandmother how to turn leftovers into a whole new dish. That carried over with me and my kids, the leftover meatloaf today would become country tacos tomorrow. I have also added a few allergen friendly recipes that I have learned along my journey.

My brother, Lonnie, and I had three goals in mind while putting these recipes together to share with you:

1. Keep it simple (KIS)

2. Finger licking good
3. Full of love

All recipes can be changed or modified to your liking.

One of the things I enjoyed most about being a culinary instructor, is teaching my students about the layers of flavoring and how incorporating different flavors, different cooking techniques to reach that lip smacking, finger licking wow moment. Though the chefs in my workshops were limited in what they could use to season their dishes, they learned valuable culinary lessons as they shopped the pantry for aromatics and ingredients for their meals.

Food Safety

I could not move forward without talking about food safety. Handling potentially hazardous food is critical, and though cooking and creating is fun, following safe food handling guidelines is key.

- Always change gloves when changing a task (after hand washing)
- Always wash all produce and vegetables thoroughly. I use a scotch-brite pad to scrub all my vegetables, potatoes and fruit, I use a two sink wash for all leafy greens
- At home it is not recommended but if you wash your poultry, always wash, rinse and sanitize your sink and all counter top surfaces. Bleach is the easiest sanitizer to use. I recommend 2 tsp. of bleach to 1 gallon of cold water.
- Always have and use a calibrated thermometer for taking temperatures
- Use your thermometer to ensure that food items are cooked to the proper temperature

Safe Minimum Internal Temperature Chart

Safe steps in food handling, cooking, and storage are essential in preventing foodborne illnesses. You may not be able to see, smell or taste harmful bacteria that may cause illnesses. In every step of food preparation, follow the four guidelines to keep food safe:

Clean – Wash hands and surfaces often.
Separate – Separate raw meat from other foods.

Cook – Cook to the correct temperature.

Chill – Refrigerate food promptly.

Cook all food to these minimum internal temperatures as measured with a food thermometer before removing food from the heat source. For reasons of personal preference, consumers may choose to cook food to higher temperatures.

Product	Minimum Internal Temperature & Rest Time
Beef, Pork, Veal & Lamb Steaks, chops, roasts	145 °F (62.8 °C) and allow to rest for at least 3 minutes
Ground meats	160 °F (71.1 °C)
Ham, fresh or smoked (uncooked)	145 °F (62.8 °C) and allow to rest for at least 3 minutes
Fully Cooked Ham (to reheat)	Reheat cooked hams packaged in USDA-inspected plants to 140 °F (60 °C) and all others to 165 °F (73.9 °C).
Product	Minimum Internal Temperature
All Poultry (breasts, whole bird, legs, thighs, and wings, ground poultry, and stuffing)	165 °F (73.9 °C)
Eggs	160 °F (71.1 °C)
Fish & Shellfish	145 °F (62.8 °C)
Leftovers	165 °F (73.9 °C)
Casseroles	165 °F (73.9 °C)

Sanitizer – make sure you use sanitizer wipes or a mixture of 2 tsp. of bleach with 1 gallon of water to clean all surfaces in the kitchen

The following pages contain recipes that are allergen friendly. Always vet all ingredients, read labels carefully and when in doubt always air on the side of caution. Call the manufacture, if an ingredient list is vague or you have any doubt about its contents.

The foundation for soups, broths and sauces, is an allergen friendly stock which can be used for any recipe.

Big Ma's Vegetable Stock

Ingredients

- To one gallon of water add:
- The peel of one white potato
- The peel of one sweet potato
- The peel of two red skin potatoes
- 1 bundle of rainbow carrots
- 1 parsnip
- 8 ounces fennel

- 4 or 5 cloves of garlic
- 8 ounces domestic white mushrooms
- 8 ounces baby bella mushrooms
- 8 ounces crimini mushrooms
- 1 to 2 sprigs of fresh rosemary

Directions

Add all ingredients to a 6 quart stock pot. Bring to a boil and then reduce heat. Simmer stock for approximately two and a half hours. Strain stock using a strainer with cheese cloth (rinse cheese cloth prior to using under cold water).

Place stock in the refrigerator or freezer (preferred) until it reaches 41 degrees.

Serves 4

One of my favorites, I like cucumbers and the combinations are endless, and I love the texture and taste of the different ingredients is this dish. Serves four.

Ingredients

- 1 English Cucumber
- 3 or 4 Parisian Cucumbers
- 1 or 2 Regular Cucumbers
- About 3 ounces thinly sliced red, yellow and white onions
- About 2 ounces of fennel
- 3 or 4 fresh garlic cloves chopped
- zest from 1 lemon and 1 lime

- juice from 1 lemon and 1 lime
- 2 to 3 ounces of cilantro
- Hint of fresh basil
- Kosher salt, black pepper and cayenne pepper to taste
- Optional - add sliced avocado just before serving

Directions

Peel the english and regular cucumbers, leave the Parisians peel on, cut the cucumbers into bite size chucks or sliced – either will work. Add to salad bowl

Thinly slice onions, fennel and garlic and add to salad bowl

Using a potato peeler, remove thin layers of skin from the lemon and lime, being careful not to go too deep into the white portion of the lemon and lime, or it will be bitter. Using a sharp knife cut the zest into thin strips, add to the salad bowl

Cut the lemon and lime in half and squeeze the juice into the bowl. Rough chop the basil and cilantro and add salt, black pepper and cayenne pepper to taste, and stir to mix all the ingredients. I like to make the salad a day ahead to allow the flavors to blend.

Note: For a heartier salad for lunch or dinner add diced chicken or beef

What a beautiful way to bring flavors and textures together.

Serves four.

Ingredients

- 8 ounces shredded napa cabbage
- 8 ounces shredded green cabbage
- 8 ounces shredded purple cabbage
- 8 ounces roasted brussel sprouts
- 4 ounces thinly sliced white or yellow onion (I like the flavor of onion so I use yellow, white and purple when I make this salad)
- 4 ounces chopped swiss chard or you can substitute purple or green kale

- 4 ounces shredded carrots
- 4 ounces celery root
- 1 cup brown sugar
- ½ cup cider vinegar
- ½ cup sunflower or olive oil (grape seed oil is an option if your oil choices are limited)
- ¼ cup of water
- Salt and pepper to taste

Directions

Add all vegetables to salad bowl. In a separate bowl mix brown sugar, cider vinegar, sunflower oil, water, kosher salt and black pepper to taste. Mix thoroughly and adjust seasoning as needed. Add to vegetable bowl and toss. Allow the salad to sit for a few hours or overnight before serving, as this will give the flavors time to blend.

Note: For a heartier salad for lunch or dinner add sliced chicken or beef (shown in photo)

ROASTED VEGETABLE QUINOA SALAD WITH CHOCOLATE CHIPS

Winner of the

Serves 4

Ingredients

- 1 cup rainbow quinoa

- 12 ounces yellow squash, sliced lengthwise into ¼ inch pieces
- 12 ounces zucchini, sliced lengthwise into ¼ inch pieces
- 8 ounces asparagus
- 4 ounces carrots, peeled and sliced lengthwise into ¼ inch pieces
- 4 ounces parsnip, peeled and sliced lengthwise into ¼ inch pieces
- 4 ounces shallots
- 4 ounces fresh garlic
- Olive oil
- 6 ounces Pasha Organic Bitter Sweet Dark Chocolate Chips
- Kosher salt and black pepper to taste

Directions

Rinse quinoa thoroughly under cold running water. In a small pot add approximately 2½ cups of water or Big Ma's vegetable stock, or any allergen friendly vegetable stock. Add 1½ cups of rainbow quinoa and bring to a boil, then reduce heat to simmer. Simmer for about five minutes, turn off heat, cover and let stand until all liquid is absorbed.

Wash all vegetables thoroughly. Add sliced yellow squash, zucchini, carrots and parsnips to a large mixing bowl. Add shallots, garlic and olive oil and toss to coat vegetables.

Pre-heat oven to 425F, place all vegetables on a sheet pan and roast for about 30 minutes, remove from oven and allow to cool for about 30 minutes.

Dice yellow squash, zucchini, carrots and parsnips. Cut asparagus into bite sized pieces and add to a medium salad bowl. Dice shallots and garlic and add to mixing bowl. Add quinoa and toss gently, season to taste with salt and pepper.

The salad should be served warm, add chocolate chips and toss. Serve quickly.

(aka the Ashley Crunch)

Serves 4

My daughter has been involved in sports her whole life, therefore she has always lived a fairly healthy lifestyle. Though she was never a picky eater, she never liked "wimpy" vegetables, so we had to improvise when it came to vegetable dishes. One of her favorite vegetable dishes we called the Ashley Crunch. This dish can be served alone or you can add meat to create a savory main dish.

Ingredients

- 1 pound bok choy cut on a bias

- 1 pound purple cabbage shredded
- 1 pound green cabbage shredded
- 1 chopped or shredded carrot
- 1 chopped or shredded parsnip
- 8 ounces mushrooms (I love baby bellas, oyster and domestic white)
- 1 ounce fresh celery root
- 1 ounce fresh turmeric

- 4 ounces chopped garlic sliced
- 4 ounces red onion thinly sliced
- 4 ounces white onion thinly sliced
- 4 ounces yellow onion thinly slices
- 1 pound sliced beef (optional)
- 1 pound sliced chicken (optional)
- Salt and pepper to taste
- Olive oil

Directions

If adding beef or chicken, cook meat first and set aside. Add 1-2 ounces of olive oil to medium sized sauté pan on medium heat, add onions and garlic and cook 2-3 minutes. Add carrots and parsnips and continue stirring 2-3 additional minutes. Add cabbage, bok choy and remaining ingredients. Stir to incorporate all flavors 3-5 minutes. Add salt and pepper to taste.

Serves 4

Ingredients

Any vegetable will do, but some of my favorites are:

- 1 quart Big Ma's Vegetable Stock (page 57)
- 4 ounces julienned celery root
- 2 ounces fresh turmeric
- 4 ounces chopped baby kale
- 4 ounces julienned parsnip and carrots
- 4 ounces enoki mushrooms (any mushroom can be substituted)
- 2 ounces olive oil
- Salt and pepper to taste

Directions

Prepare all vegetables and set aside. In a sauce pot heat oil. When hot add all vegetable and sauté for five minutes – this will bring out the flavor. Add vegetable stock all at once – this will deglaze the pan. Simmer on low heat for about 20 minutes.

One thing I learned from Big Ma was layers of flavoring. Growing up those flavors were limited yet Big Ma used the resources at hand, and we rarely saw her use a recipe.

Serves 4

Ingredients

- 1 quart Big Ma's Vegetable Stock (page 57)
- 1 cup coconut milk unsweetened
- 1 pound diced potatoes
- 1 ounce chopped fennel
- 4 ounces diced onion
- 8 ounces coarse chopped cauliflower
- 8 ounces coarse chopped broccoli
- 1 ounce chopped fresh ginger
- 1 - 2 ounces of chopped green onions for garnish
- Salt and Pepper to taste
- Olive Oil

Directions

Rinse all vegetables and herbs under cold water before cutting. I like to use a scotch brite pad to help remove dirt from potatoes.

Place diced potatoes in a small pot and add water to cover. Bring to a boil, remove from heat and set aside.

In a sauce pan on medium heat add about one ounce olive oil. When hot, add onions and fennel, cook gently for about 2 minutes. Add chopped cauliflower, broccoli and potatoes and stir to incorporate, add stock and coconut milk and allow to simmer for 15-20 minutes or until potatoes and vegetables are tender. Season with salt and pepper to taste.

Optional – If you want a thicker broth, dissolve one to two ounces of cornstarch (source to ensure it is allergen friendly) in water and add to chowder, simmer until thickened.

Growing up on government assistance my grandmother rarely threw anything away, leftovers would last several days and often became a totally different dish. When using your imagination leftovers can turn into an amazing meal. All the items used in this dish were leftovers.

Serves 4

Ingredients

- 12 ounces leftover ground beef previously used for tacos, seasoned with salt, black pepper and cayenne pepper to taste
- 4 ounces of chopped onions
- 1 ounce chopped garlic
- 2 cups leftover Quinoa (same amount if cooking fresh). If cooking fresh add 2 cups quinoa to seasoned water to cover, bring to a boil, turn off heat, cover and let stand for approxiametly 10 minutes or until all liquid is absorbed
- 1 cup tri colored canned beans
- 1 cup fresh or frozen corn
- 4 ounces chopped tomato
- 1 quart Big Ma's Vegetable Stock (page 107)

Directions

Add ground beef, onions and garlic to a sauce pot and reheat stirring constantly for about five minutes, add quinoa, beans, corn and chopped tomatoes. Continue stirring to Incorporate, add stock all at once, bring to a boil and then reduce to a simmer. Simmer on low heat until thoroughly heated.

Chicken or any other meat and vegetable can be substituted.

Serves 4

Utilizing the leftover pieces of cauliflower from the Cauliflower Rice, add stock and seasonings and you turn scrapes into Bon Appetite. I love the color that you get by adding purple cauliflower.

Ingredients

- 12 ounces white cauliflower (break into pieces)
- 12 ounces purple cauliflower (break into pieces)
- 12 ounces chopped carrots
- 6 ounces chopped onions (I love the flavor of white and purple mixed together, so I add 3 ounces of each)
- 1 clove fresh minced garlic
- 7 cups of vegetable stock (reserve 1 cup to adjust consistency if needed)

Directions

Add all ingredients to a medium bowl, toss with olive oil, salt and pepper to taste. Place on a sheet pan or roasting pan and place in 400 degree oven for about 20 minutes, or until brown in color. Add roasted vegetables and pan sauce to a soup pot, and add stock. Bring to boil and then reduce to simmer. Simmer until all vegetables are tender about 30 minutes. Blend all ingredients with an immersion blender if available, or blend in an upright blender until smooth, adjust seasoning and add reserved liquid to desired consistency.

Serves 4

Ingredients

- 16 ounces fresh cauliflower (can use frozen if available) be sure you check the label
- 8 ounces of minced rainbow carrot
- 2 ounces shallots
- 1 ounce fresh garlic
- 1 to 2 ounces olive oil
- Kosher salt to taste
- Pepper to taste

Directions

If using fresh cauliflower, use a standard vegetable grater to grate the cauliflower into pieces, set aside. Mince the carrots, shallots and garlic and set aside.

Add 1 to 2 ounces of olive oil to a sauté pan and heat over moderate heat. Add shallots and carrots and cook briefly, add cauliflower and sauté for about five minutes stirring constantly, remove from heat and serve.

Serves 4

Ingredients

- 4 - 6 ounce boneless chicken breast
- Salt, pepper to taste (I added paprika to my seasoning mix for taste but can be omitted)

For the Sauce:

- 1 cup So Delicious Coconut Milk (dairy free unsweetened)
- 1 - 5 ounce container So Delicious Vanilla Yogurt
- 1 Tablespoon Sun Butter
- 2 ounces minced shallots
- 1 ounce minced fresh garlic
- 1/2 ounce chopped fresh Sage
- Pinch of chili pepper flakes (for this recipe I used simply organic chili pepper flakes)

Directions

Add chicken to a small bowl, add olive oil and seasoning. Mix well. Place seasoned chicken on a baking pan and bake until chicken reaches an internal temperature of 165F degrees.

To a medium sauce pan over low heat add shallots and garlic, do not add oil, just warming them up and bringing out the flavor, add coconut milk and yogurt. Stir until warm (do not allow to boil) when warm add SunButter Crunch and stir until smooth, and the sauce has thickened. Add remaining ingredients and stir until thoroughly mixed. Spoon sauce over chicken and serve.

(aka the Kendall Burger)

At South Point we make our burgers fresh, they do not include seasonings or preservatives. Our meat consists of 50% brisket and 50% chuck mixed together. It is extremely important that you read labels and ask questions. If possible, find a butcher that you trust and have the ground beef mix made fresh, or you can check your grocery store's meat department. Serves one.

Ingredients

- 2 fresh ground beef burger patties – for the original Kendall burger there is absolutely no seasonings added, and is served with just the patties and cheese. Modify appropriately to your specific allergen
- 2 freshly sliced pieces of cheddar cheese (contains dairy)

Directions

Cook burger to desired doneness using a dedicated pan

Note: Garnish is optional. For Kendall, the burger is served without garnish.

Serves 4

Ingredients

- 4 - 5 ounce Flat Iron Steaks
- 16 ounces mushrooms (I like to mix and match, any mushroom will do)
- 1 cup julienne sliced onions
- Salt and pepper to taste

For the Sauce:

- 1 cup So Delicious Coconut Milk (dairy free unsweetened)
- 1 - 5 ounce container So Delicious unsweetened Vanilla Yogurt
- 2 ounces Organic Better Than Beef Bouillon Beef Base
- 1 Tablespoon Sun Butter Crunch
- 1 ounce minced fresh garlic

Directions

Preheat broiler. Rub each steak with olive oil to coat, season with salt and pepper. Broil steaks 10-15 minutes for medium – a few minutes less or more, depending on how you like your meat cooked.

Add olive oil to a sauté pan, heat oil and add mushrooms and onions. Cook 5-10 minutes until golden brown deglaze the pan with a ¼ cup of cooking wine (stock can be used in place of wine).

To a medium sauce pot add the garlic and sauté 2-3 minutes just to warm them up, do not add oil or allow to brown. Add the coconut milk and beef base; stir until the base is dissolved, add yogurt and Sun Butter Crunch, stir until smooth, do not boil.

Top steaks with mushrooms and onions, spoon sauce over steaks and serve.

(aka Chunky Chunky)

I had the honor of cooking for the 2015 Children's Heart Foundations Camp Mend a Heart. Not knowing all the children, and which allergens each child had, I was challenged from the very first day. Wanting to embrace all of the campers, and their multiple allergies, my volunteer teen chefs mentioned all kids love tomato sauce. We found all the tomatoes we could, and the adventure began. But with very limited knife skills, we donned this dish the Chunky Chunky. Making this was fun and easy, our motto for most items requiring the use of a knife was chop it and drop it in the pot.

Ingredients

- 1 pound Roma tomatoes roughly chopped
- 1 pound domestic tomatoes roughly chopped
- 1 pound tomatillos roughly chopped
- 8 ounces chopped garlic
- 8 ounces chopped onions
- Fresh basil roughly chopped
- 12 ounces gluten free pasta (we used corn and rice blend pasta)

Directions

Rinse tomatoes, tomatillos, onions and garlic under cold running water. Core and roughly chop the tomatoes and tomatillos.

In a medium sauce pot add a touch of olive oil, sauté chopped onions and garlic gently for 2-3 minutes just to release the flavor, do not brown. Add tomatoes and tomatillos all at once and mix well. Bring mixture to a boil and reduce to a gentle simmer. Allow the sauce to simmer and break down for about ninety minutes stirring occasionally. Thirty minutes before the sauce is done add chopped basil.

In a separate pot bring salted water to a boil, add pasta and cook 11-15 minutes until done, drain and serve.

Having Chef Keith in charge removed allergen worries from our shoulders. The Children's Heart Foundation runs a cost free medically supervised summer camp which allows children 7-18 with heart conditions to come and just be kids, in 2015 we had a number of food allergies and reached out to Chef  *Norman to see if he would oversee the Food Program for Camp Mend a Heart. The kids and parents already have enough to worry about. Having Chef Norman in charge with his knowledge and experience with food allergies was the perfect fit. Camp was amazing and the, feedback and appreciation from the staff, kids and parents for a worry free four days, three safe allergen friendly meals a day was overwhelming.*

Carrie Beckstrand and

Camp and Activities Director Gracie McDonough

MEET THE NEIGHBOR - 89123
Keith Norman

By Callie Thomas

Date of article - 2013

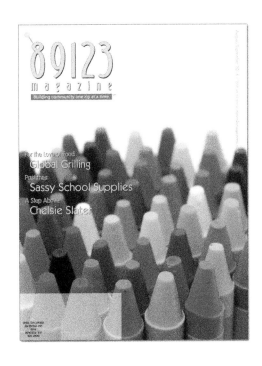

An attention to detail, a vast ability to match flavors, textures and aromas coupled with mad kitchen skills and topped with a dash of panache are the attributes of today's culinary ninjas. Chefs have come a long way baby—becoming an everyday fixture in our homes, through our computers, smart phones, Ipads and other devices to entice us with the recipe of the day. Chefs are like rock stars, filling stadiums of eager fans hungry to become wizards in their own kitchens. While there is much discussion about the culinary process, there is less discussion on how foods may be vital to one person and detrimental to another. 89123 resident Keith Norman is a rock star. Not just because he is an accomplished Las Vegas Chef of over 20 years, having shared his expertise and delicious dishes at the Mirage, Treasure Island, Paris, Suncoast and South Point. Or that he imparts his knowledge as a Culinary Instructor at the Art Institute of Nevada. Keith Norman's a culinary rock star because he's also trained to help save lives.

A passion for cooking began in Norman's grandmother's kitchen, where at a young age he learned the basics and a few tips and family recipes. He joined the Marine Corp at 18 where his duties also included cooking. "I grew up in Chagrin Falls Ohio, where community events were a way of life," he said. "So being involved in the community and especially with groups like STOP (Stop Food Borne Illness) and FAAN (Food Allergy Anaphylaxis Network) is an honor."

After leaving the Marine Corp, Keith was able to bring his considerable sense of discipline and passion to his business and the culinary world. That passion has been focused on food safety and sanitation which is an everyday part of his work as an Assistant Executive Chef for the South Point Hotel & Casino. He is also dedicated to training and educating students and culinary professionals on one of the most important facets of the food service industry. "As a Chef I can directly make a difference in lives of every guest," says Norman, who has the credentials to back it up.

In addition to being trained through the FDA in the area of food borne illness investigation, special processes, agro-terrorism and food systems disasters, Keith is a certified HACCP manager, NEHA certified food trainer, NRA certified food safety trainer and a certified registered OSHA trainer and a master certified food executive. Armed with all the necessary expertise, Chef Norman became a committee member for FAAN, a Board Member for FAACT and has been a guest speaker at annual conferences. He is honored to have been one of the first Chefs to receive an award from the FAAN organization.

More than 12 million Americans have food allergies. The incidence is highest among children. An estimated 3 million in the U.S. have food allergies. FAACT has continued to be an influential force in providing education and support to the many parents who need help managing food allergies. The organization raises public awareness, provides advocacy and education and helps to advance research. "I'm blessed, my kids Ashley and Matthew are healthy and I don't take that for granted," he said. "After meeting some of the families last year, the decision to come off the sidelines and get in the game was easy."

Chef Keith Norman continues to give back to the community by lending support to other organizations including STOP and the Children's Heart Foundation in memory of his goddaughter who passed away from a heart condition.

Comments

I am indeed pleased to read the article on Keith Norman. I had Keith in a Food Service class for three years in high school. He was an asset for me and a very charming individual. I didn't realize he had such advanced training. Thanks for the article.

Mrs. Lockert

I have the privilege of working with Chef Norman. I have never met a person so down to earth, and so passionate and knowledgeable. Kudos to you my friend.

Keith

Keith Norman [Photo: Chelsea McManus]

KEITH NORMAN'S FAVORITE MOM-AND-POP RESTAURANTS

Wednesday, September 11, 2013, by Susan Stapleton

Sin City is home to a lot of restaurants and bars, but there are tons of hidden gems that the majority of Las Vegans aren't unearthing. To help guide us to these potential discoveries, we've enlisted some of our city's food players to share their recommendations for a weekly feature dubbed Dining Confidential. Know a chef who wants to share some top dining spots? The tip line is open.

Chef Keith Norman has a passion for food safety and sanitation. After all, he's the Assistant Executive Chef and Food Safety Manager at South Point and a culinary arts instructor at The International Culinary School at The Art Institute of Las Vegas, both of which make training and educating students and culinary professionals an important facet of his jobs. He has worked his way up the culinary ladder at Bally's Las Vegas, the Mirage, Treasure Island, Paris Las Vegas, Suncoast and South Point over the past 20-plus years.

While at South Point, Norman implemented an allergen program to ensure guests with food allergies have the same enjoyable experience as diners without allergies. In fact, the hotel is hosting more than 500 guests with allergens during the 2013 Food Allergen Bloggers Conference event and Food Allergy Research and Education Walk in November. "Everyone involved in the dining experience at South Point Hotel has been certified and trained in all areas of food allergen-awareness," Norman says.

Norman also was just honored by the Nevada Environmental Health Association Executive Council as the Outstanding Nevada Environmental Health Professional of the Year Award. Here Norman shares some of his favorite mom-and-pop restaurants in Las Vegas.

Which restaurants do you turn to when you're not working?

Sunset Grill, Tuscany Grill in Henderson and Sweet Addiction.

What dishes are most memorable?

Sunset Grill has a Double Bird Burger with one chicken burger patty and one turkey burger patty served on toasted ciabatta bread. The burger is loaded with melted Swiss and provolone cheeses and topped with crispy bacon, lettuce, tomato, chipotle mayo and jalapeños. It is a must try item on the menu!

Tuscany Grill serves a rigatoni broccoli with tender onions and fresh broccoli served with a light tomato sauce and topped with pine nuts. It has a little bit of a kick to it that creates the perfect meal.

Sweet Addiction has taken the ice cream cookie sandwich concept to a whole new level. You can custom create your own ice cream cookie sandwich with homemade cookies that are made fresh every morning. The best combination I have made is with a chocolate brownie cookie and mint ice cream. The deliciously rich chocolate brownie cookie complimented with the crisp cool taste of mint ice cream is out of this world!

Why do you enjoy going there?

I have always been a fan of mom-and-pop restaurants and that is exactly what Sweet Addiction is. It has created a sweet vision that is unlike any other ice cream concept in the nation. The team at Sweet Addiction has perfected combining the wonderful and nostalgic taste of homemade cookies, all baked fresh from scratch every day, with the smooth taste of ice cream. Each time I go there, I always find a way to create a new ice cream sandwich from the 13 different cookies and 24 flavors of Thrifty brand ice cream.

http://vegas.eater.com/archives/2013/09/11/keith-normans-favorite-momandpop-restaurants.php

SOUTH POINT HOTEL, CASINO & SPA

Arizona Gaming Guide | September 2013 | azgamingguide.com

Featuring 2,200 guest rooms, South Point Hotel, Casino & Spa overlooks the famous Las Vegas Strip and the serenity of the surrounding mountains. Guests visiting South Point can experience affordable luxury through a casino offering top-of-the-line gaming technology, over 2,500 slots and more than 60 table games.

Their race and sports book section features separate viewing areas for both horse racing and general sporting events. Plus, there's eight sessions of bingo every day, a wide variety of dining options, including award-winning Michael's Gourmet Room, the world-class Costa Del Sur Spa and Salon, a barber shop, a fabulous 400-seat showroom with headlining entertainment, a 16-screen Cinemark movie complex, a state-of-the-art 64-lane bowling center, and a 165,000 square foot convention center. In addition, South Point holds one of the finest event facilities in the country with the South Point Arena and Equestrian Center, which features more than 1,200 climate controlled stalls and plays host to some of the country's most unique events.

Located less than 6 miles south of the last casino on the famous Las Vegas strip, South Point guests can easily find the property right off of Interstate 15 at the intersection of the Silverado Ranch Road and the Las Vegas Boulevard. Voted The Best of Las Vegas by the Las Vegas Review-Journal 2013 Poll in five categories, including Best Paying Slots, Best Video Poker, Best Bingo, Best Bowling, and Best Gourmet Room for one of their restaurants Michael's, guests are always assured a combination of high quality gaming excitement and exceptional customer service in this word-class casino and hotel.

In addition to the amazing casino, the excellent restaurants, the beautiful hotel where each oversized guest room features state-of-the-art LED televisions as well as Wi-Fi with high-speed internet connections, the world-class entertainment, and all of the additional amenities available at South Point, their Food and Beverage department sets the bar extremely high for customer service and guest expectations. Not only is practically every imaginable dish in almost any cuisine available at any of their nine restaurants, but their staff, led by Assistant Executive Chef and Food Safety Manager, Keith Norman, can make any dish allergen free for any patron requiring a specialized diet!

Food allergies are becoming an increasing problem in the United States and across the world. More and more, casino patrons are walking into restaurants asking for gluten free and other dietary restrictions while others avoid eating out because of possible food allergens. Based on the overwhelming response we received on our recently published article on gluten-free dining at Arizona's casinos (AZ Gaming Guide, July 2013), we wanted to highlight South Point Hotel & Casino for their dedication to food allergy sufferers. South Point is one of the only casinos we've encountered that is more than equipped to provide patrons with food allergies—for a complete casino gaming experience!

As Las Vegas is one of the top culinary cities in the world, and with the high quantity of restaurants to choose from, visitors that suffer from food allergies often experience high anxiety when deciding on which restaurant to place their personal safety. Luckily for those Las Vegas visitors with food allergies, South Point Hotel & Casino's Assistant Executive Chef Keith Norman has spent a large portion of his culinary career devoted to practicing and teaching allergen awareness cooking techniques. With over 20 years of culinary experience, Chef Norman has made it his mission to implement a world-class allergen program to ensure guests with food allergies have the same enjoyable experience as the diners without allergies.

We had the opportunity to interview Chef Norman about food allergy sufferers and South Point's allergen program:

Why is allergen-awareness important to you?

While I don't personally have food allergies, some of the tragic stories you hear that could be avoided with proper care are so heartbreaking. It's easy for me to take this issue seriously after hearing how difficult a life with food allergies truly is. For example, I had the pleasure of meeting a 16-year-old competitive figure skater, Kendall Hollinger, last year at an allergen event. After hearing she was allergic to more than 95 percent of foods and many airborne allergens, I knew I wanted to help. I told Kendall and her family about the allergen program at South Point and invited them to dine with us. Due to the severity of her allergies, this was the first time in more than 11 years that Kendall was able to dine outside the comfort of her own home. Since meeting Kendall, she and her family have dined with us on multiple occasions.

How are your restaurants allergy-friendly?

Our restaurants are equipped with a special allergen kit that is purple and easily recognizable in the daily chaos of the kitchen. It consists of everything imaginable needed to properly prepare food from cutting boards, knives, measuring utensils and more. Even tickets generated through our point of sales system with allergen specific food orders are a different color than those of customers without food allergies to avoid any mix ups. Once the kit is used, it's properly cleaned in order for it to be ready for the next allergy-friendly meal preparation.

Are there special allergy-friendly menus?

All menus are easily modified, so when customers tell us they have an allergy, the chefs will custom-create any menu item the customer would like to order. Our menus are more like a blank slate so every special dish is prepared in an allergen safe area to make it just as enjoyable as the original dish. The products are all stored and monitored to ensure there is absolutely no cross-contamination in each kitchen.

How many patrons make use of the offerings?

All of our customers with food allergies take advantage of this service. We've spent a lot of time making plans to cater to each of our guest's allergies. We have gained great buzz within food allergy awareness groups too. This year, we're hosting more than 500 guests at South Point Hotel during the 2013 Food Allergen Bloggers Conference event and Food Allergy Research and Education Walk in November.

What makes you certified to instruct others on allergen-awareness?

When I'm not at South Point, I spend my time educating culinary professionals and students about the importance of culinary safety and sanitation at The International Culinary School at The Art Institute of Las Vegas. I've trained through the Food and Drug Administration in topics like foodborne illness investigation, agro-terrorism and food systems disasters. In addition, I have certifications from the National Environmental Healthy Association, Nevada Restaurant Association, Hazard Analysis and Critical Control Points and Occupational Safety and Health Administration and I'm an active chair member on the Food, Allergy Research and Education board.

For more information on South Point Hotel & Casino or their allergen program, visit SouthPointcasino.com.

SOUTH POINT CULINARY STAFF FEARS NO FOOD ALLERGIES

Name: Keith Norman
Company: South Point Hotel, Casino and Spa
Title: Assistant Executive Chef / Food and Safety Manager

Please describe your business:

South Point Hotel, Casino & Spa has never been a traditional Las Vegas property. The South Point Hotel has always been focused on the city as a whole and how it can benefit from the role we play within the community.

South Point Hotel features more than 2,100 hotel rooms, 11 restaurants including the award-winning Michael's Gourmet Room and more than 60 table games and a race and sports book area featuring separate viewing areas for both horse racing and general sporting events; the world-class Costa Del Sur Spa and Salon; a fabulous 400-seat showroom featuring headliner entertainment; a 16-screen Cinemark movie complex; a state-of-the-art, 64-lane bowling center; and a 165,000 square foot convention center.

My role within South Point is to be a key contributor to the success of our dining offerings. Within that spectrum, I have spearheaded our property's allergen awareness program and made great strides in helping South Point really lead the way when it comes to large hotel properties focusing on food allergies.

In addition, South Point holds one of the finest event facilities in the country with the South Point Arena and Equestrian Center, which features more than 1,200 climate-controlled stalls and plays host to some of the country's most unique events. The South Point has a unique ability to cater to a large variety of niches, and at the end of the day our customers are like family and our main focus is making the experience as prosperous and stimulating for all those who visit the property.

Explain how you keep people with allergies safe.

We've spent a lot of time creating this program for the culinary staff. Every person involved in the dining experience is properly trained in food safety awareness. Our entire culinary staff, including servers, managers, hosts, dish washers, chefs, food preps and more, is required to attend our Allergen Training program and Steward Workplace Safety Awareness program every year. In addition, we mandate all chefs, managers and superiors have ServSafe Certification Training.

I've trained through the Food and Drug Administration in topics such as foodborne illness investigation, agro-terrorism and food systems disasters. I have certifications from the National Environmental Healthy Association, Nevada Restaurant Association, Hazard Analysis and Critical Control Points and Occupational Safety and Health Administration.

For example, Kendall Hollinger, a 16-year-old competitive figure skater, is allergic to more than 95 percent of foods and many airborne allergens. After meeting Kendall I knew I had to do something for her and I invited her family to South Point for dinner. Because of our allergen program, Kendall and her family were able to dine outside the comfort of their own home for the first time in 11 years. Over the past four years, Kendall and her family have stayed at South Point and dined out on many occasions at our restaurants.

Talk about the award you just won.

Once a year, the Nevada Environmental Health Association Executive Council honors one individual with the "Outstanding Nevada Environmental Health Professional of the Year Award." We have routine health inspections and it was the Southern Nevada Health District Inspector who nominated me for the award. The award is given to one individual who has demonstrated outstanding safety and health initiatives over the past year. It was quite the honor.

What are some examples on how you've implemented your allergen program to make sure your guests are safe?

Our restaurants are equipped with a special allergen kit that is purple and easily recognizable in the daily chaos of the kitchen. It consists of everything imaginable needed to properly prepare food from cutting boards, knives, measuring utensils and more. Even the tickets generated through our point of sales system with allergen specific food orders are listed in a different color than those of customers without food allergies to avoid any mix ups. Once the kit is used, it's properly cleaned for it to be ready for the next allergy-friendly meal preparation.

All menus are easily modified, so when customers tell us they have an allergy, the chefs will custom-create any menu item the customer would like to order. Our menus are more like a blank slate; every special dish is prepared in an allergen safe area to make it just as enjoyable as the original dish. The products are all stored and monitored to ensure there is absolutely no cross-contamination in each of our kitchens. We can generally adapt to food allergies on the fly, but we will also prepare special menus for those costumers with allergies who contact us with advance notice.

What's new (and newsworthy) with you and/or your company?

Earlier this year, South Point secured an eight-year partnership with the United States Bowling Congress (USBC) to build a $35 million dollar world-class tournament facility at

South Point in a deal that is anticipated to inject millions into the local economy. South Point broke ground on the facility's new expansion project scheduled to open in the summer of 2014. The multi-million dollar expansion will be more than 100,000 square feet and include two new climate-controlled arena areas planned to be housed in the Priefert Pavilion. All of this development means more people through our doors and an even stricter standard when it comes to food safety and allergen awareness on property.

What challenges do you face doing business here?

One of the biggest challenges we face, along with any dining establishment, is that regularly our guests do not inform us of their allergens. While we are certified and prepared for any situation, we are not able to successfully meet our diner's needs if we do not know of the diners allergens.

What's the best part about living in Las Vegas?

Las Vegas is one of the top culinary cities in the world, and with the high quantity of restaurants, we have the opportunity to really build awareness of the severity of allergens. In addition, it provides us the opportunity to really make an impact on the community by expanding our allergen program.

Since we have implemented our allergen program, we have gained great buzz within food allergy awareness groups. At the beginning of November, we hosted more than 500 guests at the South Point Hotel during the 2013 Food Allergen Bloggers Conference event and Food Allergy Research and Education Walk.

What do you do after work?

When I'm not at South Point, I spend my time educating culinary professionals and students about the importance of culinary safety and sanitation at The International Culinary School at The Art Institute of Las Vegas. In addition, I assist with various nonprofit organizations to educate today's youth on making nutritional decisions and I am an active chair member on the Food, Allergy Research and Education (FARE) board.

How do you think food safety will change in the coming years?

I think it will continue to gain more prominence as groups such as FARE and grass roots food allergy bloggers continue to raise awareness. Locally, all schools were recently required to have Epi-pens in every single classroom which was a huge win for the food allergy fight. These are the moves that save lives and I think the more people who showcase the seriousness of food allergies, the more people will understand the need for advanced safety techniques.

Are food allergies on the rise? Why?

Currently, more than 15 million people in the United States, including one in 13 children, are affected by food allergies. While we are becoming more aware of this serious ailment, it is an ongoing cause that needs to be severely addressed.

BREATHE EASY THROUGH MEDIA PLANET'S "ASTHMA & ALLERGY AWARENESS" CAMPAIGN

New York, NY (PRWEB) May 05, 2014

Media Planet Publishing, today announces distribution of its second cross-platform edition of "Asthma & Allergy Awareness", a campaign that aims to inspire readers to take action in supporting and practicing asthma and allergy safety. In partnership with industry leaders, the campaign provides readers with educational insight about the advancements that continue to propel the industry forward and make living through allergy season a breeze.

The print component of "Asthma & Allergy Awareness" is distributed within today's edition of The Washington Post, in the D.C. metro area, in observation of National Asthma & Allergy Awareness Month, with a circulation of approximately 450,684 copies and an estimated readership of 1.3 million. Its original digital site is distributed nationally through a vast social media strategy and across a network of top news sites and partner publisher outlets reaching an additional three million potential readers. To explore the digital campaign, visit asthmaandallergynews.com.

The publication has united the leading organizations and advocates in the asthma and allergy industry to motivate millions of readers on what the industry can offer to better manage their loved ones and their own asthma and allergy symptoms. Far too many asthma and allergy patients continue without proper education – this campaign will present them with the brands to turn to in order to breathe easy! Alongside thought leaders such as Steve Carell, James Reynolds, Chef Keith Norman, American College of Asthma, Allergy and Immunology (ACAAI), AAAAI, The Food Allergy Bloggers, FARE, Snack Safely. com, DC Asthma Coalition and NADCA along with a variety of inspiring industry leaders such as Friedrich Air Conditioning, Blue Air North America, Allergy & Asthma Network Mothers of Asthmatics, ALK-Abello, Nestle Nutrition Institute, and more.

About Media Planet

Media Planet is the leading independent publisher of content-marketing campaigns covering a variety of topics and industries. We turn consumer interest into action by providing readers with motivational editorial, pairing it with relevant advertisers, and distributing it within top newspapers and online platforms around the world.

Press Contact: Amy Jacob 646-922-1417 | amy.jacob@mediaplanet.com

Appearance on Wednesday, November 26, 2014

1. Where does your commitment to environmental health and creating a food allergen safe environment come from?

While Chef Keith doesn't personally have food allergies, he has heard many tragic stories from those that do suffer from allergies. After hearing how difficult a life with food allergies truly is, he felt very seriously about using his resources and passion to help others that suffer from food allergies.

2. What makes you certified to educate others on food allergen awareness and safety?

When Chef Keith is not at South Point, he spends his time educating culinary professionals and students about the importance of culinary safety and sanitation at The International Culinary School at The Art Institute of Las Vegas. Chef Keith is trained through the Food and Drug Administration in topics like foodborne illness investigation, agro-terrorism and food systems disasters.

In addition, he has certifications from the National Environmental Healthy Association, Nevada Restaurant Association, Hazard Analysis and Critical Control Points and Occupational Safety and Health Administration. In addition, he is an active chair member on the Food Allergy, Research and Education board.

3. What is the Food Allergy, Research and Education organization?

Food Allergy, Research and Education (FARE) is a nonprofit that was formed in 2012 as a result of a merger between the Food Allergy & Anaphylaxis Network and the Food Allergy Initiative. The nonprofit works on behalf of 15 million Americans that suffer with food allergies ranging from minor to those at risk for life-threatening allergies.

4. Tell us about your work with the Food Allergy, Research and Education board.

Chef Keith participates in a variety of conventions, fund raising events and seminars to gain support for those who are affected by allergens. Chef Keith's work with the Food Allergy, Research and Education organization has led him to design and implement a food allergen program at South Point designed to cater to every diners allergen needs.

5. What are some examples on how you've implemented your allergen program to make sure your guest are safe?

South Point's restaurants are equipped with a special allergen kit that is purple and easily recognizable in the daily chaos of the kitchen. It consists of everything imaginable needed to properly prepare food from cutting boards, knives, measuring utensils and more. Even the tickets generated through the property's point of sales system with allergen specific food orders are listed in a different color than those of customers without food allergies to avoid any mix ups. Once the kit is used, it's properly cleaned for it to be ready for the next allergy-friendly meal preparation.

All menus are easily modified, so when customers mention that they have an allergy, the chefs will custom-create any menu item the customer would like to order. South Point's menus are more like a blank slate; every special dish is prepared in an allergen safe area to make it just as enjoyable as the original dish. The products are all stored and monitored to ensure there is absolutely no cross-contamination in each of our kitchens. South Point's culinary team can generally adapt to food allergies on the fly, but will also prepare special menus for those costumers with allergies who contact us with advance notice.

6. How do you create an allergen program?

Chef Keith and South Point have spent a lot of time creating an allergen program for the culinary staff. Every person involved in the dining experience is properly trained in food safety awareness. The entire culinary staff, including servers, managers, hosts, dish washers, chefs, food preps and more is required to attend our Allergen Training program every year. In addition, it is mandated that all chefs, managers and superiors receive Servsafe Certification Training.

7. Are food allergies on the rise? Why?

Currently, more than 15 million people in the United States, including one in 13 children, are affected by food allergies. While we are becoming more aware of this serious ailment, it is an ongoing cause that needs to be severely addressed. Some states have put laws in place requiring training, signage and a reminder on the menu. However, it is not a Nevada law just yet but as part of the South Point commitment we have these rules in place here.

8. What are the most common things people are allergic to?

There are certainly many food related items that have caused allergic reactions. The top eight allergies that people are most commonly affected by include peanuts, tree nuts, dairy, eggs, shellfish, fish, soy, gluten or wheat.

EPICUREAN CHARITY FOUNDATION

Inspired Dining Series
Chef Keith Norman, Assistant Executive Chef
Silverado Steak House, South Point Hotel Spa and Casino

Featured as the first Inspired Dining Series event, a collection of dining experiences in conjunction with the Epicurean Charitable Foundation (ECF) to discuss food, mentorship and the future of Hospitality in Las Vegas, it was alongside Assistant Executive Chef and Food Safety Manager for the South Point Hotel & Casino Keith Norman that dinner was enjoyed at Silverado Steakhouse. This Old Vegas room torqued by Chef John Romine proving to be far better than many locals might have ever guessed.

Chosen for the first of these meals, thanks to both Chef Norman's contributions as a Mentor and South Point Director of Food Operations Michael Kennedy's position as Chairman of the ECF Board, was a group of five including one local Mentee that the group was greeted by a pleasant hostess and led to a table towards the back of the room. The space, which is decorated with hand painted murals and vintage photographs, is elegant yet comfortable as patrons of all ages and demographics were seen smiling over plates of both innovative seasonal options and traditional Steakhouse fare.

Embracing the old way of doing things in terms of service, the potatoes loaded and salads tossed tableside, it was over the course of nearly two-and-a-half hours that Keith, a young mentee named Ben and three others shared stories and opinions about the current state of the industry and how Chef Norman got his start cooking in his Grandmother's kitchen. He and four of his brothers are all Chefs and Keith himself a Marine Corps veteran who came straight to Las Vegas and landed a spot at Bally's where "Chef Warner – that old-time Chef who gave me my first shot, he took me through the paces from Graveyard to Swing shift to Days."

Enjoying three styles of warm bread from Great Buns Bakery and a glass of house Wine with appetizers, the underage mentee abstaining and keeping a good distance from the glass throughout the night, it was over an amuse composed of both King and Blue Crab with only a bit of filler that stories about Keith's time opening The Mirage were remembered. "A great 'wow' moment working with Mr. Wynn and Certified Master Chef Gustav Mauler" was cited as an inspiration to do things the right way; the same way Silverado cooks their tender Mushrooms in Burgundy Wine with Garlic and composes the Caesar Salad topped with Dressing with a bold smack of Worcestershire Sauce and Anchovy Paste.

Making almost everything possible on-site for nearly ten years since moving from Suncoast to South Point, Chef Norman stating "I'm not a mover and a shaker, if I'm with a good company I'm gonna stay." It was while further discussing his time at the Mirage and then Treasure Island that he first suggested passion as the most important thing a youth can bring with them to the industry, "because if you aren't passionate you're just spinning your wheels," a memorable bit of truth recalled between bites of Barbeque Prime Rib 'Tacos' served on crispy Won Ton Shells.

Enjoying dinner during Las Vegas Restaurant Week, the Chicken Vesuvio cooked in sweet Wine with Artichoke Hearts and Mushrooms is a crowd pleaser befitting a Casino described as having "a local feel." It was here that Chef Keith spent some time discussing how a background of discipline benefitted him and contributed to his world view and his reasons for working with the Epicurean Charitable Foundation. "Right after I graduated from boot camp, I was out on my own, right out in the world so I had to grow up quick. One of my first bosses in the Marine Corps was just that kind of guy – took me under his wing and taught me the things I needed to learn. Those are the kind of things I try to give back."

Noteworthy for setting a high standard in Allergy awareness, every restaurant on the South Point property deemed allergen friendly and recently winning "a national award for the best Allergy Program through a company called AllerTrain." The South Point's Food Safety Manager went on to say that he became interested in such things while teaching students for nine years at the Art Institute. "So when ServSafe was mandatory, a lot of the properties who knew I taught food safety reached out to me."

Thoroughly enjoying a clever plate called the "Filet Trio," a trifecta of Steak Medallions served on toasted Bread beneath house made Sauces, it was as the group carved up the 16oz Dry Aged Rib Eye that Keith went on to say, "I've never believed that Health 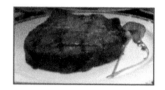 Departments should have to make us do what we as Chefs should be doing anyway." He followed up by saying, "We really have to raise the bar – protect the A." His parting advice to Ben was to treat "every day as a learning experience and never forget that."

Certainly not planning to skip Dessert after such a meal, though the lack of an on-site pastry kitchen does mean most items are imported from elsewhere save for the best-selling Beignets and Vodka-spiked Dark Chocolate Ice Cream served with seasonal Berries, it was with a smile that Ben stated "there is not an  employee on the property who won't mention how good Chef Keith's attitude is or how passionate he is." As dinner was finished with Coffee alongside Sticky Toffee Pudding and a Warm Apple Crumb Cake, the contended crowd departing on Chef Norman's advice that "if you can maintain [a positive] attitude and make sure that everyone is better in your presence you're going to go a long way."

ALLERGEN AWARENESS MONTH - MORE FOX 5

Every year we celebrate Asthma and Allergen Awareness month in May. Chef Keith is often asked to participate in getting the word out by visiting different local television shows. Fox 5's More Local Las Vegas, which is a daily show focusing on what's going on in Las Vegas, is one of his usual stops.

We are proud to be involved in educating people about allergen awareness, and take great pride in participating in these shows.

If you would like to view our own Chef Keith on Fox 5's More Local Las Vegas, visit the urls below:

http://www.fox5vegas.com/video?autoStart=true&topVideoCatNo=default&clipId=13344384

http://www.fox5vegas.com/video?autoStart=true&topVideoCatNo=default&clipId=13344196

FOOD ALLERGY AWARENESS - RESTAURANT LEGISLATION

Allergy Aware Chefs

Chef Keith Norman is a Food Allergy & Anaphylaxis Connection Team board member. He is the Assistant Executive Chef and Food Safety Manager for the South Point Hotel & Casino and an instructor at The International Culinary School at The Art Institute of Las Vegas. He trains students and culinary professionals on food allergy awareness. He was a speaker at FAACT's 2016 Food Industry and Research Summit and FAACT's Teen Conference and fed the teens with over 20 food allergies.

Chef Keith Norman's Quotes about Restaurants and Food Allergies

"Feeding food allergic guests is daunting but doable. Restaurants should be proactive and partner with their food allergic patrons. There is no excuse for not having tools in place to ensure that an allergen guest can safely dine in your restaurant."

"Restaurant staff should consider the possible consequences: fatalities, lawsuits, negative press, and how they would feel if they hurt or killed someone's child."

"Improved communication and food allergy education is critical to ensure the safety of the growing number of allergic patrons."

"Keys to success are: creating an allergen aware culture, empowering the team on all levels, leading by example, and consistent and sustained training."

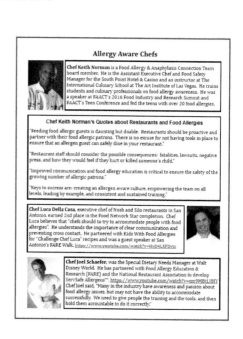

Wow. That really is incredible. I mean, I knew we were the best, but to receive the recognition is spectacular. Where are we going to hang it?

Ryan Growney
General Manager, South Point

Discipline is key. What you permit is what you promote. The South Point is blessed to have Chef Keith at the helm of this program and it is our good fortune to be known as a hotel that caters to allergen guests. Those with food allergies deserve to have a great tasting and safe meal just like everyone else. Chef Keith's constant training, coaching and sharing of unfortunate allergen incidents around the world puts real faces to those incidents and gets our employees to be "all in" as it relates to these matters. On behalf of everyone at South Point we thank you for the recognition.

Michael Kennedy
Director of Food
South Point Hotel, Casino, and Spa

STATEWIDE RESTAURANT LEGISLATION

Restaurant Laws in Illinois, Maryland, Massachusetts, Michigan, Rhode Island, and Virginia

Massachusetts and Rhode Island became the first states in the U.S. to pass legislation related to restaurants and customers with food allergies.

Under the new laws, restaurants are required to display a food allergy awareness poster in the employee area. Restaurants are also required to place a notice on their menus (or menu boards, etc.) asking customers to inform the restaurant if anyone in their party has a food allergy.

Finally, and perhaps most importantly, the new laws require certified food protection managers (i.e., restaurant managers and/or senior employees) to receive food allergy training via a video, and obtain a certificate showing that they have received the training.

Learn more about the state laws:

- Illinois

   Illinois law, HB2510, was signed into law on August 25, 2017. Amends the Food Handling Regulation Enforcement Act. Provides that all food service establishments shall have at least one certified food service sanitation manager who has undergone training that follows nationally recognized industry standards for allergen safety and allergen awareness available on the premises at all times that the food service establishment is in operation. Provides that all individuals seeking food service sanitation manager certification or food service sanitation manager recertification shall undergo training that follows nationally recognized industry standards for allergen safety and allergen awareness. Provides that any costs for the allergen safety and allergen awareness training shall be borne by the individual seeking the training. Effective immediately.

- Maryland

This bill requires that, beginning March 1, 2016, restaurants request that patrons with known food allergies notify the employee taking the customer's food order of the allergies prior to ordering food. The bill also requires DHMH to establish online lists of (1) approved food allergen awareness training courses and accredited tests and (2) resources about food safety and food handling related to food allergies.

- Massachusetts

The Act Relative to Food Allergy Awareness in Restaurants (FAAA) was signed into law by Governor Patrick in January 2009. The purpose of the Act is to minimize risk of illness and death due to accidental ingestion of food allergens by increasing restaurant industry and consumer awareness of regulations and best practices with respect to major food allergens.

The Act requires that certain food establishments comply with regulations developed by the Massachusetts Department of Public Health (MDPH) that will include provisions for the prominent display of a food allergy awareness poster in the staff area of food establishments, a notice on menus for consumers with food allergies, and additional food allergy training for certified food protection managers. The FAAA also requires the Department to develop a program for restaurants to be designated as "Food Allergy Friendly" (FAF) and to maintain a listing of restaurants receiving that designation on the Department's website. Participation in the FAF program will be voluntary. The Department has asked that a representative from local health be added to the workgroup for designing the FAF guidelines and requirements for restaurants to receive the designation. The requirements will include, but not be limited to, maintaining on the premises and making available to the public, a master list of all the ingredients used in the preparation of each food item available for consumption and strict adherence to procedures that prevent cross contamination.

- **Michigan**

Michigan law was signed into law in January 2015 and requires certified food safety managers in most restaurants to take a training course with an allergen awareness component.

- **Rhode Island**

The director of health shall establish a food allergy awareness program which shall require that every food-service establishment shall: (1) Have prominently displayed a poster approved by the director relative to food allergy awareness in the staff area. The poster shall provide, but not be limited to, information regarding the risk of an allergic reaction and shall be developed by the department of health in consultation with the Rhode Island hospitality association and at least one representative from a quick service restaurant; (2) Include on all menus a notice to customers of the customer's obligation to inform the server about any food allergies. The director shall develop and approve the language of the notice in consultation with the Rhode Island hospitality association and at least one representative from a quick service restaurant; and (3) Designate a manager who shall be knowledgeable with regard to the relevant issues concerning food allergies as they relate to food preparation. The director shall prepare and provide both written and video materials for mandatory review by persons designated as managers of any food-service establishment, or the persons designated as managers shall be certified by a food protection manager certification program that is evaluated and listed by a conference for food protection-recognized accrediting agency as conforming to the conference for food protection standards for accreditation of food protection manager certification programs. The department of health shall include knowledge of food allergy issues as part of the certification procedure for managers in food safety pursuant to chapter 21-27 of the Rhode Island general laws.

- **Virginia**

  Virginia law, HB2090, was signed into law in 2015. Regulations of the Board governing restaurants shall include but not be limited to the following subjects: (i) a procedure for obtaining a license; (ii) the safe and sanitary maintenance, storage, operation, and use of equipment; (iii) the sanitary maintenance and use of a restaurant's physical plant; (iv) the safe preparation, handling, protection, and preservation of food, including necessary refrigeration or heating methods; (v) procedures for vector and pest control; (vi) requirements for toilet and cleansing facilities for employees and customers; (vii) requirements for appropriate lighting and ventilation not otherwise provided for in the Uniform Statewide Building Code; (viii) requirements for an approved water supply and sewage disposal system; (ix) personal hygiene standards for employees, particularly those engaged in food handling; (x) the appropriate use of precautions to prevent the transmission of communicable diseases; and (xi) training standards that address food safety and food allergy awareness and safety.

FAACT will advocate for statewide restaurant legislation. If you are interested in advocating in your state, please Contact Us.

Great opportunities to help others seldom come,
but small ones surround us every day.

Sally Kock